The Heart of the Prophetic
Workbook & Study Guide

THE [HEART] OF THE PROPHETIC

Workbook & Study Guide

Unlocking the Prophetic Through Understanding
The Father Heart of God

IVAN ROMAN

ISBN-13: 978-1537420691
ISBN-10: 1537420690

Edited by: Angela Hughes
Cover Design by: Nikki Haken
Interior Design by: C. Rayne Warne

www.empoweredlifechurch.org
www.ivanroman.org

ENDORSEMENTS

ely do I get excited about a "new" prophetic book, because most of them lack "new." Ivan Roman's new book
henomenal! Turn off your smart phone, sit down for two hours, and strap yourself in for a mindset-changing
ok. Even if you have been a Charismatic for years, you will find this book filled with surprising gems.

. JONATHAN WELTON
lton Academy Supernatural Bible School
st-selling author of *School of the Seers*
w.weltonacademy.com

n Roman is a prophetic teacher, a good prophetic teacher, and his book *The Heart of the Prophetic* captures
s. There is a new generation of leaders talking about walking out the prophetic ministry and lifestyle journey,
I Ivan is a voice you need to listen to. Ivan combines excellent theological perspective with gripping stories,
I you will grow as you take part this great resource.

AWN BOLZ
thor of *Translating God, Keys to Heaven's Economy, Growing Up With God*
w.bolzministries.com

n is a pursuer of God and the things of God. Since I first met him at BSSM, I have been impressed with this
aracteristic. This book is an expression of that and it invites the reader into that journey for themselves. *The
art of the prophetic* is great teaching on the prophetic, but it is more than that, as it is really equipping the be-
ver with a life of hearing God, leading and ministering out of that. I know the man and I know his God, and I
mmend this man to you. I invite you to hear God more as a result of this helpful practical and inspiring book.

UL MANWARING
thel Church, Redding CA

ighly recommend my good friend Ivan Roman's new book called *The Heart of the Prophetic*. This is more then
good read! It's a heavenly blueprint to moving in greater realms of intimacy and breakthrough in the things
God. In this book you will learn how to soar to new heights in the realm of The prophetic as well as hearing
od's voice. Be inspired as you read and discover the Fathers love and heart for your life which will in turn un-
ck your identity and launch you into your destiny.

RAME and MIRANDA NELSON
ving At His Feet Ministries
thor of *Burning Ones: Calling Forth a Generation of Dread Champions, Encountering Angels,* and *Manifest-
g God's Love Through Signs, Wonders, and Miracles: Discovering the Keys of the Kingdom*

I have known Ivan Roman and his prophetic journey for many years and have personally seen his accurate prophetic gifting and character touch countless lives. I know his new book on *The Heart of the Prophetic* will equip and ready you to live a true prophetic lifestyle and release the word and heart of God.

TODD BENTLEY
Fresh Fire USA
Author of *The Reality of the Supernatural World, Journey into the Miraculous,* and *Christ's Healing Touch Vol.*

I have known Ivan Roman as a friend and minister for many years, and have seen a man of great honor and trust. His new book *The Heart of the Prophetic* is a must read for anyone desiring inspirational truth and revelation teaching. Ivan has operated in the prophetic gift for many years, and has taken his experience and the Word God and molded them together in a practical and revelational way. He truly carries a prophetic gift for "such time as this," and I encourage anyone interested and/or ministrering in the prophetic to read this book.

BRENT BORTHWICK
President/Founder of Windword Ministries
Senior Leader of Windword Churches

DEDICATION

ting a book is not a one person job. The time and people it takes to see a book from start to finish is more
n most realize.

ant to first and foremost thank my beautiful wife Erica. It's hard enough to put up with me, let alone when
consumed with a project from God. Erica you are my constant support and friend.

my three boys, Isaiah, Aren and Ezra. My prayer is that you would understand the heart of our Father toward
h of you, and walk in intimate friendship with Him.

Angela Hughes for editing, transcribing and encouragement along the way.

ould also like to thank Dr. Jonathan Welton for blazing a trail with New Covenant teaching. The church is
ter off because of you.

tly, I would like to thank Empowered Life Church for believing in me. You guys rock!

TABLE OF CONTENTS

INTRODUCTION

I often wonder what it would be like to walk with Jesus on the shores of the Sea of Galilee. I could have nessed Him performing miracles, witnessed the unrecorded events in scripture, witnessed how He treated ple, and maybe the tone in which he spoke to people. We read scriptures and can easily misinterpret them ause of our experience, or our filter of theology. I am convinced that Jesus was more than a miracle worker, or ologian. Jesus being fully God and fully man is the embodiment of love itself. The bible doesn't say only that d loves, but that God is love. The more I walk with Jesus, the more I am convinced of His goodness and love.

Religion has not done the greatest job revealing Christ from the scriptures. Many in the church have led for a life less than Christ has purchased for us at the Cross. For this reason, I believe the Father is rising a people that will rightly represent Him on the earth. He is rising up a prophetic people that carry not only the s of the Spirit that break the chains of discouragement, but a people that model the very heart of the Father d a Christ like life.

Historically, we have seen many moves of God come and go. Very often the personalities of the catalysts larger than life, and many of the moves of God have ended because of some sort of compromise in the life of minister. A desire for the power of God without knowing the person of God will always lead us into the sin pride. This phenomenon has caused people to not pursue walking in the fullness of the normal Christian life.

The scripture teaches us that "faith works through love" Galatians 5:6. Those who love the most will not ly see the greatest faith released on the earth, but also the greatest long lasting fruit.

"In this is my Father glorified that you bear much fruit." John 15:8NIV

I am convinced that when the love of God is allowed to flow through our hearts by the Holy Spirit, we ll see a generation represent Christ to the world with love, truth and grace. We have yet to see a generation lk in radical giftedness and radical love; however there is a promise that "the glory of the latter house shall greater than that of the former" Haggai 2:9. The scripture does not teach that the generation is greater, but ply, that the glory will be greater. The thought of a generation walking in greater glory than Moses or even vid may sound arrogant, but Hebrews declares:

"These were all commended for their faith, yet none of them received what had been promised, since God had planned something better for us so that only together with us would they be made perfect." Hebrews 11:39-40 NIV

The destiny of these heroes of faith will not be complete until we finish what they started, and we cannot complish this without His glory and presence. This is astounding! This is why this generation needs to take iously the mandate of heaven. The mandate to preach the gospel to all creation while walking in radical love, d in wholeness in our relationships.

My prayer is that we allow the Spirit of God to shape us into containers that can carry the fullness of God. ontainers that bear the fruit of His Spirit, and do the greater works Jesus prophesied would be released through All of this being produced out of walking in intimate fellowship with God.

[Section One]
The Nature and Character of God

Lesson 1
The New Covenant

The way we perceive God will affect the way we communicate to Him, and to people. The more time spend with Jesus, and His word, the greater we begin to understand His nature properly. Much misrepresentat of God has come from those who do not have clear understanding of the covenant we are under, which Hebr says is "a better covenant with greater promises" Hebrews 8:6. God has never changed, but His covenants v men have. In scriptures we see God had made a covenant with Abraham (Genesis 15:18), Noah (Genesis 9: David (2 Samuel 7:13), and Moses (Exodus 19-24). But the scriptures also say that when Jesus was crucified, shed blood created a *New Covenant*, Luke 22:20.

The covenants God made with Abraham and David where eternal covenants we see fulfilled in Christ.

"The record of the genealogy of Jesus the Messiah, the son of David, the son of Abraham…" Matthew 1

Christ fulfilled the Abrahamic Covenant.

"Now the promises were spoken to Abraham and to his seed. He does not say, 'And to seeds', as referring many, but rather to one, 'And to your seed', that is, Christ." Galatians 3:16

Christ fulfilled the Davidic Covenant.

"Your house and your kingdom shall endure before Me forever; your throne shall be established forever. Samuel 7:16

Jesus is seated forever on the throne of David, fulfilling God's promises to David. The Mosaic Covena however, was not eternal and had a shelf life:

"For Christ is the end of the law for righteousness to everyone who believes." Romans 10:4

This is important because most people are hindered in their relationship with God because they are con-
tly conscious of their sin, and feel unworthy to enter the presence of the Lord. The *Mosaic Covenant* prom-
that if you were able to obey, then you where blessed, but if you disobeyed you where cursed (Deuteronomy
The *New Covenant* that was made in Christ, is not based on blessings and curses, but is based in sonship.
ist is the end of the curse of the law, making us all sons and daughters (Galatians 3:13).

The promise of the *New Covenant* is that our sins will be remembered no more, and that Christ has made a
for us beyond the veil. This is almost the complete opposite of what was promised in the *Mosaic Covenant.*

"If we want to know what the Father is like we have but to look at Jesus"

If we want to know what the Father is like we have but to look at Jesus. Jesus declared, 'I and the Father are
', and when Phillip asked to see the Father, Jesus responded, 'Phillip how long have I been with you, and you
show us the Father?' Jesus is the expressed image of the Father (Hebrews 1:3).

A very important verse to completely understand God's heart for His people is found in Exodus:

*"'You yourselves have seen what I did to the Egyptians, and how I bore you on eagles' wings, and brought
you to Myself. Now then, if you will indeed obey My voice and keep My covenant, then you shall be My own
possession among all the peoples, for all the earth is Mine; and you shall be to Me a kingdom of priests and
a holy nation.' These are the words that you shall speak to the sons of Israel."* (Exodus 19:4-6)

God's original intention for His people was that they would minister directly to Him as a kingdom of priests.
d was inviting all of His people to hear His voice and to serve Him directly.

*"All the people perceived the thunder and the lightning flashes and the sound of the trumpet and the moun-
tain smoking; and when the people saw it, they trembled and stood at a distance. Then they said to Moses,
"Speak to us yourself and we will listen; but let not God speak to us, or we will die."* Deuteronomy 20:18-19

The people feared hearing God's voice and requested a mediator. This changed the covenant offer God
d made with His people. From here on you'll notice there's no longer an invitation to all of the children of
ael to hear His voice, but the Levites are raised up to represent the Lord.

Prior to this experience on Mt. Sinai, God dealt directly with His sons and daughters. After this event, a
ediator and new laws were put into place. In order to live an empowered life, it's critical to have a healthy view

of the nature and character of God, or we will approach God like we are at Mt. Sinai, instead of Mt. Zion.

"Unlike your ancestors, you didn't come to Mount Sinai—all that volcanic blaze and earthshaking r ble—to hear God speak. The earsplitting words and soul-shaking message terrified them and they beg him to stop. When they heard the words—"If an animal touches the Mountain, it's as good as dead"— were afraid to move. Even Moses was terrified. No, that's not your experience at all. You've come to Mc Zion, the city where the living God resides. The invisible Jerusalem is populated by throngs of festive an and Christian citizens. It is the city where God is Judge, with judgments that make us just. You've com Jesus, who presents us with a new covenant, a fresh charter from God. He is the Mediator of this coven. The murder of Jesus, unlike Abel's—a homicide that cried out for vengeance—became a proclamatio grace." Hebrews 12:18-21 MSG

"I pray for us all to have fresh eyes to see the Father through the blood of Jesus. As I have shared the revela of God found in the New Covenant, and God's original intentions for us, I have witnessed people exhale say, 'Now I can trust the Father!'"

Covenant Names of God

Now we are going to explore the Covenant Names of God. I feel it is important in understanding God's ture that we know what He is called.

Yahweh

The first time God reveals His name in scripture is found in Moses' encounter at the burning bush.

"Then Moses said to God, "Behold, I am going to the sons of Israel, and I will say to them, 'The God of y fathers has sent me to you.' Now they may say to me, 'What is His name?' What shall I say to them?" C said to Moses, "I AM WHO I AM"; and He said, "Thus you shall say to the sons of Israel, 'I AM has s me to you.'" God, furthermore, said to Moses, "Thus you shall say to the sons of Israel, 'The Lord, the G of your fathers, the God of Abraham, the God of Isaac, and the God of Jacob, has sent me to you.' Thi: My name forever, and this is My memorial-name to all generations." Exodus 3:13-15

God reveals Himself to Moses as 'I Am Who I Am'. Rabbinic traditions teach that God breathed as He spc His Name. In this He was revealing Himself as a living, breathing, talking God who always was, always is a always will be. Our life and walk with God should be like breathing. The scripture teaches us that in Him we l and move and have our being. This reveals so much about the nature and character of God.

He is not the God who *was*, He is the God who *is*. He is present, consistent and ever present. God will always what the word of God says He is.

It's so refreshing to me to know that I can count on the nature of God to be consistent. He may change His d but He doesn't change His nature and ways (Exodus 32:14). There are nine *Compound Names* of God, each reveals the different parts of God's nature:

ovah Nissi – *"The Lord My Banner"* Exodus 17:8-16

God is our Victor. The Lord is the banner of victory over our battles. When we are facing battles in our life, member God is our banner.

ovah Raah – *"The Lord is My Shepherd"* Psalms 23

When we are in need of protection, provision and guidance, we can take comfort that God is our shepherd.

ovah Rapha – *"The Lord that Heals"* Exodus 15:22-26

In every covenant, the one constant is that the Lord heals His people of sickness and disease. When the ene-tries to afflict us, we can put our hope in the healing power of God.

ovah Shammah – *"The Lord is There"* Ezekiel 48:35

We are also told in the New Testament that we are the temples of the Holy Spirit where God's presence des. When we feel alone, we call upon the Lord who is there.

ovah Tsidkenu – *"The Lord Our Righteousness"* Jeremiah 23:5-8

Our righteousness or right standing with God is as filthy rags. It is only the Lords righteousness imparted to by faith in the cross of Jesus that we are in right standing with God.

ovah Mekoddishkem – *"The Lord Who Sanctifies You"* Leviticus 20:7-8

When we are struggling, we are to find peace that it is the Lord who sanctifies or makes holy as we agree with m.

Jehovah Jireh – *"The Lord Will Provide"* Genesis 22:1-14

Whatever we have need of, all we have to do is ask.

Jehovah Shalom – *"The Lord is Peace"* Judges 6:24

Shalom means completeness, wholeness, health, peace, welfare, safety, soundness, tranquility, prospe
perfectness, fullness, rest, harmony, and the absence of agitation or discord. When we don't know what to do
a situation this name of God has the answer.

Jehovah Sabaoth – *"The Lord of Hosts"*

All of creation, and every living creature are subject to the power of God. We in turn, as His creation, e
to love and serve Him.

By meditating on each name, we learn that God is I Am. He is ever present, and never changing. He is a C
who looks after lineages of those who serve Him, He is our victor, He is our Shepherd, He heals our disease,
is always with us, He is our righteousness, He sanctifies us, He will provide for us, He is the source of our pea
and He is the Lord who fights for us.

Reflection Questions

1. How do you feel understanding the Old and New Covenants impacts you in your walk with God?

_____

_____

_____

_____

2. Why is it important in the understanding of the nature of God, that we also know what He is called?

_____

_____

_____

_____

3. Meditate on the names of God. In what areas is God revealing His nature to you?

_____

_____

_____

_____

[NOTES]

_____

_____

_____

_____

_____

_____

_____

_____

_____

_____

_____

_____

_____

_____

_____

_____

_____

_____

_____

_____

_____

_____

_____

_____

_____

Lesson 2
The Love and Forgiveness of God

The scripture tells us that God is love. Not that God occasionally loves, but His very nature is love. Love is a y watered down word in the English language. The word love is used to describe such a vast array of emotions arding our spouses, families, pets, movies and chocolate. In the Greek language there are four words for e. They are *eros*, *storge*, *phileo* and *agape*. Here is a brief overview of the greek definitions of the word love:

- *Eros*: The greek word *eros* is where our English word *erotica* is derived from. The media continually bombards our culture to make us feel like we need to be more attractive to the opposite sex. We buy cologne, get a haircut, buy more clothes, and the list goes on. The youth are hearing a message that true love is merely a physical attraction. Obviously, it is important to be attractive to the person we marry, but physical attraction is only one aspect of love. Most of our society lives in this stage of love.

- *Storge*: *Storge* is the love found in family. The love we share with our mothers, fathers, brothers, and sisters. This is a deep love, but still not the strongest love.

- *Phileo*: This love is best described as brotherly love. Not simply as kin but the love that causes us to reach out, help our neighbor, or help the old lady across the street.

- *Agape*: When the scripture says God is love, it uses this type of love. *Agape* is the unconditional love of God. All human love has conditions, but God's love is unconditional. He loves us just because we are. We belong to Him and it's His love and goodness that draws us to Him.

  "This is how God showed his love among us: He sent his one and only Son into the world that we might live through him. This is love: not that we loved God, but that he loved us and sent his Son as an atoning sacrifice for our sins." 1 John 4:9-10

There are two points I want to develop from these passages of scripture. 1 John 4 is almost the same as John 6 which states, *"For God so loved the world He gave His only begotten Son, that whosoever believeth in Him 'l not perish but have everlasting life."*

The first point I want to observe in this passage of scriptures is that God's love gives and it gives freely. ost humans, before Christ, give with the motive to get. God gave His most precious gift to mankind to bring back to a living relationship with Him. The unselfish factor about this is that God won't force us to love Him ck. The Father has given us free will. Why wouldn't He just control us, and make us serve Him? Because true e deserves a choice.

The second point I want to observe is in verse 10 of 1 John 4, stating that God first loved us, not that we ed God. He loved us and sent His Son to be the atoning sacrifice for our sins, and this demonstrates that God he initiator of this grand love story, and would go to any length to bring us back into right relationship with m. God's desire was to have such an intimate relationship with mankind that Jesus teaches us to call God

Father. The image of an angry God dangling like a spider over the pits of hell does not rightly represent nature of God.

When we understand this truth, that it is God's love for us that compels us to love others, we understand that we ca make love happen. Through growing in our knowledge and relationship with God we also grow in love. Love is on the fruits of the Holy Spirit, and fruit grows. Love grows in us by our understanding of how much we are loved by H

> *"I heard a voice say, 'I love your presence*
> *more than you love mine.'"*

As a new believer I had an experience where I saw a scene in a garden with two flaming swords blocking way. Then the swords pulled back and I saw a hand beckon me to come and I heard a voice say," I love y presence more than you love mine." This baffled me. God loves my presence? Who is this God we serve, w loves so purely and so violently? Understanding God's love and forgiveness towards us draws us to Him

God's Love for the One

One of the best illustrations in scripture of the goodness and forgiveness of Father God is found in the of Peter. During the last supper when Jesus declares that one among them would betray Him, Peter opens mouth again, "Not me Lord!" Jesus replies, "Peter by the time the rooster crows three times you would ha denied me three times." Then Peter, consistent with his character, says "Not me God."

Peters has the amazing revelation of Jesus in Matthew 16, and then, just chapters later, is being told, "C behind me, Satan!" because he was trying to talk Jesus out of the suffering of the cross. This was Jesus' ve purpose for coming to the earth. We all know the rest of the story. Jesus is crucified and Peter fulfills the Lor prophecy and denies Him three times.

In John 20:2-7, Peter and John hear of the emptied tomb, and they both go running to the tomb. John o runs Peter. I have to wonder what Peter was thinking on the run. How horrible he must have felt for denying Messiah. John walks into the tomb first, and Peter hangs back. Now any doubt that Jesus was whom He said was is removed. Peter may have thought, "He is who He says He is and I, Peter, have denied Him not once b three times."

> *"Very early in the morning, on the first day of the week, they came to the tomb when the sun had risen. A they said among themselves, 'Who will roll away the stone from the door of the tomb for us?' But when th looked up, they saw that the stone had been rolled away—for it was very large. And entering the tomb, th saw a young man clothed in a long white robe sitting on the right side; and they were alarmed. But he so to them, 'Do not be alarmed. You seek Jesus of Nazareth, who was crucified. He is risen! He is not here. S the place where they laid Him. But go, tell His disciples—and Peter…'"* Mark 16:2-7

After Jesus was raised from the dead, an angel told those present, "Go and tell the disciples- and Peter. love how the scripture isolates Peter, as if to say, "Peter may have forgotten me but I have not forgotten Him." of heaven wanted Peter to know that God still loved him, and that He was thinking about him.

In John 21:5-7, a very interesting conversation happens between Peter and Jesus. Jesus asks Peter if he *ipao* loves Him, twice. Peter replies twice that he *phileo* loves Him. Jesus is revealing to Peter the difference in ir love for one another. The last time Jesus asks Peter if he loves Him like a dear friend or companion, Peter grieved and replies, "Lord, you know."

There are times in each one of our lives where our hearts become aware of the shallowness of our love God. This is always reflected in the way we live and the things we value. Peter denies Jesus three times. Jesus s Him three times if he loves Him. For each time Peter denied Jesus, He told Him he loved Him.

Jesus' attention to single Peter out later turns Peter into one of the greatest apostles in scripture. There comes such oneness in Peter's relationship with God that the Holy Spirit overshadows him, and everywhere went his shadow healed the sick.

> *"It's easy to believe in the love of God for the multitudes,*
> *but where we struggle is God's love towards us personally.*
> *These scriptures illustrate God's love for the one."*

eflection Questions

1. We have learned about the four Greek definitions of love. God's love is Agape love. Meditate on the definition of Agape love and see if there are any areas where you may struggle with believing God loves you unconditionally.

_____

_____

_____

_____

2. The scripture says that God's love gives, and it gives freely. It also says in 1 John 4, that God first loved us. In what areas do you struggle with feeling like you have to earn God's love, or struggle with believing that God's love is freely given?

_____

_____

_____

_____

3. This Lesson illustrated the relationship between Jesus and Peter. Jesus pursued Peter even though Peter, through his failure, tried to run away. How did this story about Jesus' love for Peter bring freedom you? In what areas have you felt like you didn't measure up, so therefore could not be loved by God?

_____

_____

_____

_____

[NOTES]

_____
_____
_____
_____
_____
_____
_____
_____
_____
_____
_____
_____
_____
_____
_____
_____
_____
_____
_____
_____
_____
_____
_____
_____
_____
_____
_____
_____
_____
_____

Lesson 3
God's Love for Me

My story, like Peter's, is one of God's mercy and of God's love. I wasn't in pursuit of God, and I really [ ] not care to know Him; however, He was in pursuit of me. As I remember back to the day the Lord saved my l[ ] I can still feel the fear and excitement of that night. It was a Friday evening, and myself along with a few of [ ] friends were going to Philadelphia to do some barhopping. We all chipped in to get a limo so we wouldn't [ ] drinking and driving. We arrived, got drunk, and at 2 a.m., received a call from our limo driver. He was stuck[ ] traffic, and he asked if we could walk to the nearest main street so he could pick us up quicker. The street t[ ] we were closest to happened to be located in a rougher section of the neighborhood. Directly across the str[ ] from where we stood waiting, there was a group of Hispanic men pushing each other around. The action be[ ] to escalate, and as the police arrived, the men took off running.

While all this action was taking place, I was standing at the end of an alleyway waiting for the limo, and [ ] ing very drunk I passed out on a yellow post that was at the end of the curb. The yellow post came up to my h[ ] and the alley way was directly to the right of me. I passed out, but then was suddenly startled by a loud noise t[ ] sounded like a loud firecracker. At that very moment I felt something grab the back of my shirt and pull me ba[ ] I felt fire go by my forearm, and instantly I heard weeping in the distance. Looking around I saw people lying[ ] over the sidewalk crying. I ran to check on my friends and they were all on the ground too. Then I heard, "[ ] hip! My hip! I'm shot in my hip!" I ran over to see what had happened, and saw an African American guy hold[ ] his hip. Someone shouted my name and I realized that the limo had arrived. I ran to it as fast as I could, jump[ ] inside, and we took off. All of this happened in a flash. I was so overwhelmed that I couldn't cry or laugh. I j[ ] put my hands over my face.

While I sat there with my hands over my face, I heard an inner audible voice which sounded like a very lo[ ] thought, "Where would you go if you died right now?" I responded, "I would die and go to hell. I'm drun[ ] Then the next thought came, "Where was that man shot?" I answered, "In his hip." Then I saw what would [ ] like a video in my mind. I saw myself lying down on the yellow post. I watched as a bullet was going directly [ ] my head, and something pulled me back so that the bullet went right over my forearm and hit another man [ ] the hip. Something had saved my life. I had an encounter with God. Needless to say, I gave my life to the L[ ] a week later.

God is a God of Forgiveness. My testimony clearly reveals a God who is in pursuit of His people. I was[ ] even looking for God. I thought religion was something people did when they got old, but what I found was[ ] religion. I found Christ. After I asked Christ to come into my heart I felt clean. I knew I was forgiven. red [ ] more.

Testimony of the Love of God

Years ago when I was attending ministry school, I worked for a state run group home for troubled teens[ ] ed this job because I had the opportunity to minister to a lot of young men.

When the boys at the group home behaved themselves, they were permitted to go on outings during the ekends. So I would take them to church. On one of those weekends I brought two of the boys, Michael and ınkie, to church when Benny Perez was the guest speaker ministering. Both of these young men were involved gang activity, and had very troubled lives. From what I had observed of them, neither of them had a relation- p with the Lord. During the service I waved the youth pastor over to see if he could have Benny Perez pray them. As it worked out, Benny Perez did come over and began to minister to them, and the power of God ıched both of them. They both fell to the ground rolling and trembling under the power of the Holy Spirit. I s shocked! I was expecting that maybe they were going to receive a word of encouragement, but this was much ter than I could have imagined.

When we got into the van to return them back to the group home, I started asking lots of questions. They th responded the same way. They made it clear that I wasn't allowed to tell anyone what had happened be- ıse they had cried.

A few weeks later, I received a phone call at 9 p.m. asking if I could report to work immediately. Almost a ın as I said yes and hung up the phone, I instantly got a migraine headache. Even on my way to the group me I got lost while driving, and hit a bird. What was going on? Something was definitely happening in the rit.

Once I had arrived there the other staff members left, and I was on duty with a staff member from Peru. We tantly hit it off sharing God stories. Some of the other boys began to overhear me telling God stories, and y all walked out with their bibles and asked if we could do a bible study. That was hard for me to turn down. ichael and Frankie were amongst the boys that had come in the room, and I asked them to share what God d done with them the night before. They looked up at me quickly, and then I realized I had forgotten that y had asked me not to tell anyone. However, Frankie said, "You can tell them". So I began to share the story, d as I did, one of the boys named Cesar said, "Man I wish today was Saturday." "Why Cesar?" I asked. "Then norrow would be Sunday, and I would be able to experience what they did."

I began daydreaming about laying hands on the boys, and then started thinking about the potential of noth- ; happening. I was beginning to be gripped with fear and unbelief. But I worked myself up into praying for :sar, and I blurted out "Stand up!" His eyes got big, and he jumped up. I told him that I was going to lay hands him, and that the power of God was going to come upon him, even though I was not believing anything uld happen. I began to pray and invited the Holy Spirit, and BAM! The presence of God began to fall upon n, and he took a few steps back. Then he sat down, and put his hands over his eyes. I asked him, "What would ıu do if someone was at the door?" He quickly responded, "I would let them in." I said," Jesus is knocking on door of your heart. Will you let him in?" And then I led him to Jesus.

The next hour was one I will never forget. I held my own revival service in a group home. We led the young ın to the Lord, prayed for the infilling of the Holy Spirit, and laid hands on one another for healing. What was xt to do? I ran to my car, grabbed a worship cd, and I taught the boys how to rest in the Lord.

One of the young men blurted out, "I'm in a garden!" So I ran over to him to interpret the experience, but he buted out, "I know what it means! Jesus wants to walk with me the way He walked with Adam in the garden."

Each young man was having his own experience with God. One of the most impactful experiences w Frankie's. He started weeping and trembling under God's power. I asked if he was ok, and he asked me if I I read his file. I told him that I had not. He then began to tell me that his mother and father were both in pri: for life. His mother, while high on drugs, drowned his baby sister in the bathtub because she couldn't get he stop crying. He went on to tell me that His grandmother became his caregiver, but one morning he walked i her room to wake her, and she had passed away in her sleep.

Tears flooded his eyes as he told me that while resting in the Lord, he had a vision. He saw Jesus stand next to his grandmother, and she was holding his baby sister. It was such an emotional moment that we e braced, and wept together.

That night after sending the boys off to bed, they were noticeably different. I sat in the staff office in disbel Then I heard a loud exhale followed by a voice saying, "You don't know how long I've wanted to touch the but I didn't have hands to flow through." The reality of those words from God gripped my heart. I will alw remember the truth that I learned that night. It is our heavenly Father's desire to touch the broken.

"If God didn't need hands and feet, He would do it all Himself, but He has chosen to partner with man."

Reflection Questions

1. In my testimony I share about how God pursued me even though I wasn't looking for him. How does t make you feel about the reality of God's love for you?

_____

_____

_____

_____

2. When I was in the group home, God began to stir in me the faith to lay hands on the boys. The first thing that began to happen was that I became overcome with fear and unbelief. As I pressed through my fear into faith, God began to do an amazing work. What are the areas in your life where you are allowing fear or unbelief to keep you from walking in your inheritance?

_____

_____

_____

_____

3. We are God's hands and feet. God has chosen to partner with man. How does that change your paradigm about mans relationship with God, and what that may look like here on the earth?

_____

_____

_____

_____

[NOTES]

[Section Two]
The Heart of a Prophet

Lesson 4
Friendship with God

"No longer do I call you slaves, for the slave does not know what his master is doing; but I have cal *you friends, for all things that I have heard from My Father I have made known to you." John 15*

In 2004 I had a visitation from the Lord while at a meeting in Homer, Alaska. My eyes were opened, an saw a brown mantle floating out of the sky. I was having an open vision, and I could see it with my natural ey The speaker at the meeting began to prophesy that he saw the Lord releasing mantles, and as he was prophesy this I could see a brown mantle shimmering and falling down. I asked the Lord what he was showing me, a then I saw an open vision of the Lord Jesus standing in front of me. The Lord spoke to me and said, "Today I c you my friend. I will make you a recognized prophet to your generation." This was one of the most life changi encounters that I have ever experienced personally. As I meditated upon the encounter, I began to ask the Lc about what this brown mantle represented, but it wasn't until some years later that He clearly brought about tl answer to me.

The answer came when I had another encounter at the graduation of a bible school I had taught at. On last day of school we decided to wash the feet of the students as a sign of humility. It was a prophetic act to s "Blessed are the feet that bring good news. Do likewise to others." And as I was washing their feet, the spiri the Lord came upon me, and I began to weep in the presence of the Lord. Then the Lord said to me, "Ivar have called you to wash the feet of the body of Christ for the rest of your life."

These two experiences have significantly impacted how I have lived as a minister of God. My life is one friendship with God, to be a prophetic voice to a generation, and to wash the feet of the body of Christ.

I began to see that the Lord was not just commissioning me, but commissioning a generation. What the Lc wants to do is raise up a people that will have an understanding that the prophetic ministry is a ministry that is wash the feet of the body of Christ. It is a ministry that is called to walk in a place of humility and servanthoc and to function out of a place of friendship with God.

"Pursue Love, and earnestly desire spiritual gifts. Especially that you might prophecy." 1 Corinthians 1

When I was younger I remember asking one of my pastors why, above all gifts, Paul says we are to purs prophecy. Why not healing? When we look at the scriptures, Jesus moved mostly in healing, and miracles. asked me, "Think about it Ivan. How do you receive a true prophetic word?" and I said, "Well, you hear the voi of God." And he said, "Exactly! So above all things, and above all gifts, desire to hear His voice, and to speak I heart. "

Humility in the heart of a prophetic minister has to be number one. We also have to have a real relationship with the Word so that we can rightly communicate the nature and character of God. Secondly, we have to have a sensitive heart to Jesus, and a genuine love for people. When the spirit of God speaks to us, He shouldn't have to yell at us. He should only have to speak quietly, and we hear. There is a passage in Isaiah that says, *"God dwells with those that are humble of heart, and that tremble at his word."* When a prophetic individual grows in the gifts of the spirit without growing in humility, this is where it becomes dangerous. The individual may start to feel like maybe they are receiving prophetic revelation because they are more anointed then everybody else, or maybe they are better than other people. They forget that the Lord can speak through the mouth of a donkey if He needs to, and the bible says even the rocks will praise him. We need to understand that as a mouthpiece for the Lord, we not only want to speak what the Father is saying, but we want to rightly reflect his heart.

In the encounter I had where the Lord was speaking to me about washing the feet of His people, and Him calling to me to be His friend, I began to realize something. In John 15:15 it says, *"I no longer call you servants, but I call you friends. For a servant doesn't know what his master is doing, but to a friend I reveal my secrets."* In the Old testament God used a lot of people. When I say used, I mean that he anointed, or His spirit rested upon them, but he called very few His friends. Abraham was a prophet, and he was called a friend of God. The bible says that Abraham looked for a city in which its builder and maker was God. So when God spoke to Abraham, he obeyed God's word. God said to Abraham, "Look at the stars and see how many your descendants will be. Look at the sands of the seashore, so will your descendants will be." Abraham began to hope beyond hope it says in Romans, and out of that faith Abraham became a friend of God. Out of Abraham's radical faith, and obedience to God, he became known as friend.

"A *friend of God will ask questions.*"

In Hebrews this scripture says, "Call unto me and I will answer you, and I will show you mysteries." Some people have those rare sovereign encounters with the Lord, and those are amazing, but then there are those that get a steady stream of revelation from God. We may begin to wonder, "What is it about those individuals that they continue to get so much revelation, while others get only the rare encounter?" I believe it comes down to the fact that a friend of God will ask God questions. In a developing friendship, you ask questions to get more acquainted with the other person. You don't just sit there and experience a friend, you interact with them. This is critical for a friendship to grow.

We are learning to develop a relationship with God through prayer, and we are learning to ask questions, but then we must also learn to listen. Psalms 46:10 says, "Be still and know that I am God". We need to learn to allow the Lord to speak back. A critical part of being in relationship with the Lord is allowing him to speak back to us, and encourage, direct and correct us. This is the place with the Lord where we learn how to worship and praise. As we 'hang out' with Jesus, we begin to glorify him, and magnify him, and begin to see him as he is.

Reflection Questions

1. God is commissioning a generation of ministers to function out of a place of humility and servant ho rooted out of our friendship with God. How does this alter the way you look at the ministry of the p phetic?

_____

_____

_____

_____

2. Why is it that out of all the spiritual gifts we should desire to prophesy?

_____

_____

_____

_____

3. What made Abrahams a friend of God as compared to so many others that were used by God in the C Testament?

_____

_____

_____

_____

4. A friend of God will ask questions. How is this important in a developing friendship with God?

_____

_____

_____

_____

[NOTES]

Lesson 5
Character, Credibility & Favor

Character

It is essential that we grow in *Character*, but we also have to have the patience and the understanding that takes time to develop that *Character*. I gave my life to Jesus at twenty years old, and before that I had a lifest with much brokenness. I had to grow in my relationship with the Lord, and grow in an understanding of sonsl and identity. There are some Christians that were raised in Christian homes, and grew up with Godly mor and values. They maybe went to church, and had experiences with God at a young age. These different life periences mean that a different level of *Character* has to be developed. *Character* is not something you can through impartation or the laying on of hands. *Character* is something that is developed over time, through trials of our lives, and growing in our personal understanding of what our triggers and hooks may be. *Charac* grows when we begin to recognize those areas that the enemy has tried to establish strongholds, and we allow Holy Spirit to do a work in our hearts and lives. In order for the Holy Spirit to do a work in our lives, we ne time building a relationship with God so that the fruit of the Spirit begins to grow. "Abide in Me, and I in yc As the branch cannot bear fruit of itself unless it abides in the vine, so neither can you unless you abide in m (John 15:4). The fruit of the spirit comes from abiding in intimacy with Jesus.

> *"We will not have influence when we prophesy*
> *if we are lacking in Character."*

We have all encountered individuals with bad character, but they can still move in power. It is usually or a matter of time before people begin to see the lack of Godly fruit coming from their lives. As ministers that a called to have influence over people, it is important that we have allowed the time it takes for God to develop c *Character*. There has to be more accountability and *Character* developed in a person who moves in influen and power, than someone who doesn't, and this takes time. We will not have influence when we prophesy, the right kind of influence, if we are lacking in *Character*. *Character* equals time.

Credibility

Credibility, just like *Character* also equals time, and a lifestyle of faithfulness. There has to be the e dence that we are walking in a fruitful and established relationship with Jesus, and this is evident when a pers is in relationship with God.

What kind of relationship do we have with the Body of Christ? It is essential and important that we have lthy relationships with man in order for *Credibility* to be established. Many times I have had traveling minis- ask if they could come and minister in my church. They always have an amazing resume to share with me, exploit to tell me about. All these things are probably true, but outside of a relationship with them, unless Lord tells me otherwise, I won't have them come and speak. The reason is because as a shepherd it is my onsibility to protect the sheep. Especially with prophetic ministers, I need to know who they are, and if they e *Character*. Are they having problems in their life, are they having marital issues, and if so, are they working them? Are they allowing people to speak into their lives? Are they a part of a local church? Do they have com- nity? These are important things to know if they are going to establish *Credibility* as ministers.

vor

"Favor Ain't Fair" – TD Jakes

The bible says of both Samuel and Jesus that they grew in *Favor* and stature with both God and man. We can w in *Favor*. It is true that God loves all of us equally, but we are not all favored the same. All you have to do is k at the scriptures to see that this is true. John was the only one that rested his head on the chest of Jesus. Often es we look and wonder why another person seems to have a greater measure of favor. David was a man after ds own heart, though he made a lot of mistakes. In Acts 13:22 it says that David accomplished the purposes of d for his generation. So David, in the midst of all his weakness, was still a man after Gods own heart.

God is the one that gives *Favor*, and this is very challenging for people to understand. It's especially hard for North American church, because we are accustomed to the 'American Dream' and pushing our way to the . We push and work our way through our education and degrees to become more successful, and then we velop an entitlement mindset that can cause the belief that we deserve all we worked for; however, this is not case with God. God grows our *Favor* with both God and Man, and this is important to understand.

It is critical that we begin to understand that we may be functioning with a Gift of Prophecy, and may have lesire to prophesy over rulers and kings, but without the *Favor* the Lord brings, we will have no platform to ease it. If God has placed a desire within our hearts to prophesy over people of influence and governments, en God will cause it to come to fulfillment. But we cannot be impatient, jealous and frustrated because no one istening to us. We have to remember that it takes time for the Lord to develop the *Character*, *Credibility* and vor that is required to have that kind of influence. We have to be able to steward the voice of God in our lives, d be willing to cooperate with the refining process that we need to go through to get there.

Reflection Questions

1. Why is it so important to have Character? And how is it that we can develop the fruit of Character in ⬚ lives?

_____

_____

_____

_____

2. Why is it important to have community and accountability to develop Credibility? How are you mak⬚ sure this is happening in your life?

_____

_____

_____

_____

3. God is the one that gives Favor. How are you positioning yourself so that the Favor of God can incre⬚ in your life?

_____

_____

_____

_____

4. Why do we need Character, Credibility and Favor to have influence?

_____

_____

_____

_____

[NOTES]

Lesson 6
Hooks and Mixture

Hooks

"Satan comes for me, but he has nothing in me"
John 14:30 NASB

We need to be a people that have nothing that the enemy can hook. When you go fishing you take bait, a in John Bevere's book, 'The Bait of Satan', he teaches that the enemy likes to use the 'bait' of offense. The e my's goal is to create an offense that causes a root of bitterness to grow, because he knows that a root of bittern defiles many. The enemy throws hooks into areas of our heart that are not yielded to the Lord, and as long as do not yield these areas, the enemy will have the ability to reel us in.

A great example of this is in the life of a man by the name of John Alexander Dowie. Dowie was known his amazing healing ministry during the early 1800's. At the height of his ministry, he was known as a man w walked in a great level of humility, and was known as a humble servant of the Lord. It is recorded that John Lake received an impartation of healing through Dowie's ministry, as well as healing for his family. Some hist books say that there were two self-proclaimed prophets that brought a prophetic word to Dowie. They said t John Alexander Dowie was the next Elijah prophesied to return. Dowie originally responded by standing up a rebuking them publically, but there was something in his heart that clung onto the word. Dowie started out ministry living very humbly, but by the end of his life he was dressing as a high priest, and was proclaiming t he was indeed the Elijah prophesied to come.

We need to take into consideration the lives of the men that preceded us like John Alexander Dowie, a how they started off walking in great humility unto the Lord; however, in the end they allowed Satan to wre havoc in their lives. If we are not yielded to the Lord, and are not walking in a continual lifestyle of repentan then the enemy will take the opportunities we give him to sow seeds that can bear bad fruit and trap peop Repentance is not just turning away from sin, but the changing of the mind.

If we want to avoid having *Hooks* in our heart, we need to learn to have the wisdom God gives us to rev what is in our heart. It's critical for our emotional health. The bible guarantees that offense will come, but you not have to choose to take offense. When we become triggered and feel angry, sad, lonely or depressed, and choose to allow ourselves to become offended, then we have positioned ourselves to become a victim that blan others for the negative feelings we have. It is our responsibility to steward the garden of our heart.

xture

When I was about 20 years old, and I had just given my life to the Lord, I went to a really inspiring men's eat. The retreat launched me into an incredible spiritual high, and caused a real hunger for the Lord to n in me. After returning from the retreat I went to a Sunday morning service. During the part of the service en they started taking the offering, people began to walk up to put money in the offering baskets, and an older nan walked past me. Instantly, I saw her completely naked in my imagination. This was so odd because she n't even a young or attractive woman to me. I physically reacted to what I had seen in my mind's eye, and put hands over my face. It was completely demonic, and I began to be overwhelmed with emotions of shame. ought to myself, "I'm not a man of God, and this whole week at the retreat was for nothing. How can I be a n of God and have these kinds of thoughts?" I felt guilt and shame attacking me, and as this was happening, elder of the church approached me. He said that he felt like the Lord told him to come over and check on . I didn't want to tell him what had been going on, but finally he got me to tell him. He smirked at me and said, "Ivan, don't you know what that is?" I said, "No!" He said to me, "I can only imagine that you had a past ore you gave your life to Christ, and now the enemy is trying to pull up some of the things you struggled with our past so that you would feel shame and guilt. That's the enemy!" He began to tell me his testimony, prayed me, and broke off the lies of the enemy. Because I had those images in my head from before I was saved, the emy was able to pull those things up, and try to use them against me.

We need to have an understanding of what it looks like to have *Mixture* in our heart if we are going to op- te in the prophetic anointing. We must learn how to yield our members to the Lord; Our members being eyes, ears, heart, mind, mouth and our hands unto righteousness. Job 33:33 says, "I made a covenant with eyes not to lust after a woman." If we have a gifting as a seer, and the Lord uses us prophetically to minister people, then we hear the voice of the Lord with our eyes. So then if we are not careful to yield our eyes unto teousness, and are not careful what we see, then the enemy can actually begin to use these things in our agination. There is a level of consecration that we have to live in, and walk in as yielded vessels if we want to nister to the people of God.

The second area where we can allow *Mixture* is in our opinions. We have so many opinions about politics l theology. If we are not careful, we may form opinions that are so strong, that when the Lord begins to speak is contrary to what we have believed, then our own opinion will begin to wrestle with the truth that God is ng to speak. This area of *Mixture* requires a sense of humility and surrender to overcome.

> *"Our job as prophetic ministers is to cover those we*
> *minister to by having integrity in our heart."*

We also have to be careful that we do not have *Mixture* in our heart because of the people we are ministering It is our job as prophetic ministers to cover those we minister to by having integrity in our heart. When we ministering prophetically over someone, his or her heart can become very open and vulnerable. Especially ur prophetic words are accurate, then their heart can begin to open to our heart. Their spirit becomes open receiving from the Lord, a hunger for the truth grows, and a hunger for hearing what the Father would say to

The Heart of a Prophet

them grows. Our gifting and callings are without repentance, and if we are living a life of compromise, then individual may be affected by that *Mixture*. Part of the prophetic word will be from the Lord, and the other might be coming from a place of hurt or offense within us.

It is so vital that we are prepared in our hearts so that when "Satan comes to me, he has nothing in me" J 14:30

Reflection Questions

1. The bible guarantees that offense will come. How do we learn to position our heart in ordered to allow offense to bear bad fruit?

_____

_____

_____

_____

2. After reading this Lesson, ask the Holy Spirit to reveal any areas where you may have offense. What the Lord show you? Write them down and take some time to repent.

_____

_____

_____

_____

3. Why is it important to not have Mixture in our hearts when ministering to other people?

_____

_____

_____

_____

[NOTES]

_____
_____
_____
_____
_____
_____
_____
_____
_____
_____
_____
_____
_____
_____
_____
_____
_____
_____
_____
_____
_____
_____
_____
_____
_____
_____
_____
_____
_____
_____
_____
_____

[Section Three]
Spirit Talk: The Language of the Holy Spirit

Lesson 7
Filter of Cessationism

One of the hindrances the church faces today in being able to clearly hear the voice of God, and ex~~p~~ence His presence, is a teaching called *Cessationism.*

The filter of *Cessationism* is a teaching that originates out of a passage in 1 Corinthians which says,

"Love never fails; but if there are gifts of prophecy, they will be done away; if there are tongues, they *cease; if there is knowledge, it will be done away. For we know in part and we prophesy in part; **but w*** ***perfect comes, the partial will be done away.***" 1 Corinthians 13:8-10

The group that teaches on the belief of *Cessationism* can be referred to as *Cessationists.* This understan~~c~~ is that the gifts will have ceased '*when perfect comes*'. Cessationist's interpretation of the word '*perfect*' in this v~~e~~ means the canonization of the bible.

There are two primary views within the teaching of *Cessationism.* The first view being, because of canonization of the scriptures, we have the bible. Now because of that fact, we no longer need the gifts of spirit because the 'perfect', representing the word of God, has come. The understanding was that the Holy S~~p~~ was moving, and moving in power, up until the canonization of scripture in AD 397, then ceased. If you st~~u~~ church history, you will see that miracles did not cease. During the dark ages, many of the desert fathers w~~ere~~ moving in the miraculous. Saint Patrick, along with so many others, walked in not only the gifts of the Sp~~irit~~ but had encounters with the living Christ. There are many testimonies of miracles after the bible was canoni~~zed~~.

The second view of *Cessationism,* is the belief that the gifts of the Spirit ceased after the death of the ~~last~~ apostle. The problem with this theology is that biblically there were 22 apostles. This theology is only taking i~~nto~~ consideration the original 12. On top of which, there is also no historical evidence of when John the Revela~~tor~~ died. The Bible says in Hebrews 13:8 that, "Jesus is the same yesterday, today and forever". So this means tha~~t~~ we just look at the Old Testament perspective, that he is a God that heals yesterday, today and forever, then ~~it's~~ biblical to see that gifts and miracles are for today.

"He is a God that heals yesterday, today and forever, so *~~w~~hen it is biblical to see that gifts and miracles are for today."*

The same Spirit that flowed through Jesus now abides on the inside of us doing the same works that Jesus while on the earth. 1 Corinthians 12 teaches us about the gifts of the Holy Spirit, and to not be ignorant of m. It then goes directly into 1 Corinthians 13 which is called *The Love Chapter*. It is in that chapter that Paul ins to teach that when the 'perfect' comes, we will no longer need prophecy, tongues and even knowledge. is is where we discover a problem in 1 Corinthians 14:1 where Paul says, "Pursue love and earnestly desire spiritual gifts, especially that you may prophesy."

Directly after teaching that there will come a time when gifts will cease, he goes on to teach on how import-it is to desire spiritual gifts, especially prophecy.

So what does it mean when Paul says, "When 'perfect' comes"? Well, that's actually simple. It is the second ning of Christ. When Christ comes we will no longer need prophecy. We will no longer need to be healed ause there will be no sickness or disease in heaven. We will no longer need words of wisdom, and we will no ger need words of knowledge because Christ has come. So that's the perfect!

We want to see the power God manifested out of love, and compassion, so that people of faith will not rest the wisdom of men. The wisdom of men being humanism and rationalism, which I believe are the god's of age. We want the wisdom of God, so that we would once again believe in the supernatural power of God.

flection Questions

1. What are the two primary beliefs within the teaching of Cessationism?

_____

_____

_____

_____

2. What does Paul mean when he says, "When *perfect* comes"?

_____

_____

_____

_____

3. How did this teaching on Cessationism impact you? Did it challenge you in any areas that you had viously believed?

_____

_____

_____

_____

[NOTES]

_____

_____

_____

_____

_____

_____

_____

_____

_____

_____

_____

_____

_____

_____

_____

_____

_____

_____

_____

_____

_____

_____

_____

_____

_____

_____

_____

_____

_____

_____

Lesson 8
Manifestation of the Gifts of the Spirit

"Now about the gifts of the Spirit, brothers and sisters, I do not want you to be uninformed." 1 Corinthians I

This scripture points out that it is almost as if the Apostle Paul knew that the *Gifts of the Spirit* would be area that would be greatly misunderstood, not only during his day, but in ours as well. Denominations have b formed and split surrounding the subject of the gifts of the Spirit, specifically the gift of tongues. Regardles what side of the fence we choose to take on the gifts, they are still in operations today, and should be apart of lives of everyday believers.

The *Gifts of the Spirit* are critical for living an empowered life. In my experience, when discussing spirit gifts in action, most believers tend to think of a church holding a revival service; however, most of my favo stories about the gifts in operation happened in the lives of everyday believers. For example, a mother mi receive a word of knowledge to help her children get break through, or a business man may receive a wor wisdom that brings direction on where he should take his business. I have even personally experienced how gifts of the Spirit have impacted my own workplace, and brought revelation to the management. It is import to understand that the gifts of the Spirit are always in operation, not just when we are at church, but in our eryday lives.

We are to have our hearts aligned with God's word, so that we properly understand what the motivation our heart should be when operating in the *Gifts of the Spirit* towards others. In times when God's gifts are u in humility and love, they bring healing, hope and encouragement to those receiving. However, when the g of the Spirit are used for selfish gain or selfish motivations, the effects can be devastating. The person receiv may have been blessed in the moment, but after a while the motives of the minister may be revealed, and in tu used to discredit the move of the Spirit.

"To one person the Spirit gives the ability to give wise advice; to another the same Spirit gives a message special knowledge. The same Spirit gives great faith to another, and to someone else the one Spirit gives gift of healing. He gives one person the power to perform miracles, and another the ability to prophesy. gives someone else the ability to discern whether a message is from the Spirit of God or from another spi Still another person is given the ability to speak in unknown languages, while another is given the abi to interpret what is being said. It is the one and only Spirit who distributes all these gifts. He alone deci which gift each person should have." 1 Corinthians 12:8-11 NLT

In this verse above, we see listed the Gifts of the Prophet. These gifts are the word of wisdom, word of kno edge and the discerning of spirits. Are you surprised that the gift of prophecy isn't found on that list? Prophecy

iously one of the gifts that a prophetic individual would operate under, but it will become clearer by the end
his chapter what is considered to be the true gift of prophecy, according to the apostle Paul. But now, we are
ng to break down the three gifts from 1 Corinthians 12.

ord of Knowledge

A *Word of Knowledge* is not human knowledge, or book smarts. A word of knowledge is a supernatural knowl-
ge from the Lord regarding someone's past or present. One of the clearest words of knowledge in Jesus ministry
ound in John 4.

> *"He told her, "Go, call your husband and come back." "I have no husband," she replied. Jesus said to her,
> "You are right when you say you have no husband. The fact is, you have had five husbands, and the man
> you now have is not your husband. What you have just said is quite true." "Sir," the woman said, "I can see
> that you are a prophet." John 4:16-18*

The word of knowledge flows in my ministry quite often partnered with the gift of healing, or the gift of
ophecy. The word of knowledge can increase faith to receive healing, and can increase the atmosphere of faith
causing people to be made aware that God knows everything about them.

ord of Wisdom

The *Word of Wisdom* reveals the mind of God for a future situation. Knowledge reveals, and wisdom directs.
e bible is filled with words of wisdom, and one example is of Jesus' word of wisdom to Peter in Matthew 26:34
ere Jesus declared that Peter would deny Him three times.

The word of wisdom is the ability to see what will happen in the future. The wisdom helps people to see what
ll happen, and often how to prepare for what is to come.

ft of Prophecy

The *Word of Wisdom* and the *Gift of Prophecy* are often confused. Most people call everything revelatory
ophetic". Prophecy carries elements of the future, and in this, the Lord will often allow the prophetic minister
see His heart as well as His plans for an individuals life. So the prophetic gift coupled with the word of wisdom
lps to give direction to the prophetic word.

This would be a good time to define the *gift of prophecy*. The word prophecy is *prophetiea*, which means to
eak for the mind and counsel of God. Prophecy is both fore-telling and forth-telling. The word forth-telling
eans to tell forth or proclaiming. A good example of forth-telling would be the preaching of a *rhema* word from

God, which is called prophetic preaching. Fore-telling, on the other hand, is predictive in nature, and can h
pen in preaching or through a public prophetic word.

The Three Levels of Prophetic Ministry

First Level of Prophecy –The Spirit of Prophecy:

There are three levels of prophetic ministry. The first level is operating under the Spirit of Prophecy. T
Spirit of Prophecy gives us all the ability to prophesy one to another so that we might learn. 1 Samuel 10:10 t
us that the Spirit of the Lord came upon Saul, and he began prophesying among the prophets. Saul comes n
the prophets, and he begins to prophesy, but Saul was not a prophet. Often times this is what happens when
gather as a group of believer's in the presence of the Lord.

This level of prophecy is available to all of us. We are all able to prophesy when the Holy Spirit pours out
prophetic anointing upon us; however, this is a specific type of prophecy. This prophecy is what Paul is talk
about in 1 Corinthians 14:3 where it says, "The purpose of the prophetic ministry is for edification, exhortat
and comfort."

Second Level of Prophecy – The Gift of Prophecy:

I Corinthians 12 talks about the different giftings that the Lord has distributed to the body of believers, a
the Gift of Prophecy is one of them. This gifting requires a greater level of maturity, and this is the maturity t
develops the *Character*, *Credibility* and *Favor* that I talked about previously. This gift flows more quickly th
others, and does not have to wait for the Spirit of Prophecy. The Gift of Prophecy will receive prophecy for p
ple and for churches within their sphere of influence or community.

Third Level of Prophecy – The Function of a Prophet:

The difference between the 1 Corinthians 12 Gift of Prophecy, and the Ephesians 4:11 Prophet ("God gi
some to be apostles, prophets, evangelists, pastors, and teachers") is platform and influence. For example, t
Lord can speak to somebody with a Gift of Prophecy regarding the president, but the president may never
that word because of a lack of favor, platform or influence. The Prophet will receive that word, and the Lord w
begin to open the doors to take that prophecy to presidents, kings, ambassadors, and rulers.

Prophetic Guidelines

The *Gifts of the Spirit* call out healing, hope and deliverance when used properly. Sadly, they aren't alw
used the way the Father intends them to be used. This may be confusing, but Romans 11:29 states that the g
and callings are without repentance. Meaning, someone can fall away from Jesus, and still move very accurat
and powerfully in the Gifts of the Spirit.

The Gifts of the Spirit should flow out of intimacy with the Lord; however, that isn't always the case:

"So then, does He who provides you with the Spirit and works miracles among you, do it by the works of the Law, or by hearing with faith?" Galatians 3:5

According to this verse, God works miracles because of faith, not good behavior or perfect character. This is [wh]y it's possible for a ministry to move in radical signs and wonders, and later found to be in compromise. Many [hav]e fallen away from the faith because of these testimonies, or attribute every miracle, word of knowledge, or [pro]phecy to the devil because a minister wasn't walking in righteousness. The truth is, the gifts aren't to make us [loo]k good, the gifts are for the people receiving the ministry.

[Di]scerning of Spirits (Eyes of God)

The *Discerning of Spirits* is one of the most needed, as well as misunderstood, gifts in the body of Christ. [Wh]en people hear the word discernment, they usually think of discerning demons in the room. Discerning de[mo]nic spirits is a part of the gift, but thankfully not the only part. Individuals with this gift can see, sense, smell, [tast]e or even touch in the realm of the spirit.

In the spirit we have five senses, the same way we have five senses in the natural. As born [aga]in believers this is true for all of us. We all have this ability, because the Spirit of God lives in [us] to discern between good and evil. There are different levels of the gifting of discerning of spir[its] just as with the gifting of prophecy. All can discern, but some are especially gifted and will [exp]erience discernment more frequently; however, we can train our senses to discern good and evil.

"But solid food is for the mature, who because of practice
have their senses trained to discern good and evil." Hebrews 5:14

[In] the Spirit we have eyes to see

Ephesians 1:18 speaks of the eyes of our heart. I have personally seen demonic spirits with my own eyes. [Th]is will often happen when the Lord is showing what might be trying to oppose someone's life, or oppose the [ch]urch I am ministering in. On one occasion, I was caught up in the Spirit and saw in a vision of a demonic spirit [pe]rched like a bird in the spirit realm. I watched as the assignment of this demonic spirit was to spit darts that [en]ded up hitting the backs of believers. In return the believers would spit darts in the back of their brothers and [sis]ters. Through this revelation, I was able to share the vision and lead the church into repentance for backbiting [an]d gossip, and it brought break through.

In the Spirit, we have ears to hear the voice of God

Revelation 2:29 says, "He who has an ear, let him hear what the Spirit says to the churches." Since Go[d]
spirit, after we are born again, our spiritual ears are open to hear the voice of God. God can speak to the un[be]
liever, and He can speak audibly or any way He chooses. For those of us who are born again, our spiritual [ears]
become like spiritual antennas that tune into the still small voice of God. As sons and daughters of God, hear[ing]
the voice of our Father becomes a part of our adoption into the family of God.

We can taste in the Spirit

Psalms 34:8, "O taste and see that the Lord is good." I have had very few experiences in discernment thro[ugh]
taste, but I have had a few. Stories that I have heard where others have discerned through taste have been sim[ilar]
to mine. In some meetings, I have experienced the taste of something foul in my mouth, almost like metal. [The]
first time I wasn't sure what I was experiencing, but after a while I started to notice that every time I would ta[ste]
this foul taste, someone would ask me to pray for them because they had cancer. Somehow the Lord allow[ed]
me, through the gift of discerning of spirits, to taste sickness. Through this discernment, I could recognize wh[ich]
people needed prayer for cancer during a meeting.

We can smell in the Spirit

*"But thanks be to God, Who in Christ always leads us in triumph (as trophies of Christ's victory) a[nd]
through us spreads and makes evident the fragrance of the knowledge of God everywhere, for we are [the]
sweet fragrance of Christ unto God, among those who are being saved and among those who are perishin[g]*
2 Corinthians 2:14-15 AMP

I have been in meetings where the room filled with the scent of cinnamon. I would ask the person next [to]
me if they could smell it also, but they often couldn't. I then began to realize I was discerning something [in]
the spirit. Different smells have come to represent different things to me, most importantly, the fragrance of [the]
Lord. I have also smelled very putrid smells when others couldn't, and at times that has been the Lord reveali[ng]
the presence of demonic or fouls spirits in the room.

A person with a gift of discerning of spirits has to be very careful to not become critical of what they see[.]
they are not careful, the Lord may be revealing something negative of someone or something to teach them h[ow]
to pray for the individual. The problem is that if the discerning person doesn't understand the reason they are d[is]
cerning a negative thing, they can then begin to improperly judge and label the individual with what the ene[my]
is attacking them with. When God reveals something that is negative, He is calling us to pray in the opposite sp[ir]
it His perfect will over that individual's life. This is where the gift of prophecy flows with the discerning of spir[its]

Take notice that this gift is to discern spirits. The gift of discerning of spirits discerns:

1. Demons

2. Angels

3. Human

4. Holy Spirit

scerning of Demons

Teaching on discerning the demonic is always tricky. I have taught this many times, and have seen people erience incredible freedom. I have witnessed people begin to understand how God reveals the strategy of the my, and how it gives them the direction they need to pray victory over their own life, or another person's life. ave also experienced people falsely accusing others, who they disagreed with or have had problems with, of ing demons because they 'discerned' them.

Paul prays that our love would abound in knowledge and discernment in Philippians 1:9-10. If we feel we ceive a demonic spirit, it's critical that we choose love in how we approach the situation.

scerning Angels

From the beginning of the bible to the end of the bible, we see encounters with angels. If it weren't for the elic realm intervening, Jesus would have been murdered long before the cross.

"Now when they had gone, behold, an angel of the Lord *appeared to Joseph in a dream and said, "Get up! Take the Child and His mother and flee to Egypt, and remain there until I tell you; for Herod is going to search for the Child to destroy Him."Matthew 2:13

Angelic visitations sent from Jesus happen today. In fact many Muslims are being converted to Christ through ions, dreams, angelic visitations and visitations from Christ Himself; however there have been many occults t have started because they had a visitation of an angel of light that preached another gospel. This is why it is tical to have a deep understanding of the word, but also to share, and allow others to test the encounters that have. Regardless of how powerful the encounter might be, if it doesn't line up with the revelation of God in ipture, then we have to learn to reject it.

Testing spirits

*"Do you believe this just because I told you I had seen you under the fig tree? You will see greater things t.
this." Then he said, "I tell you the truth, you will all see heaven open and the angels of God going up
down on the Son of Man, the one who is the stairway between heaven and earth." John 1:50-51*

From this verse we see the angels are on the earth and ascend to heaven. It makes sense that the angel
God would ascend and descend upon Jesus the Son of Man, but what about the sons of men?

I have personally met many people that have had angelic visitations, and have seen angels. I have also
angelic visitations. In my personal experience, they don't happen every day, and the encounters I do have d
last very long. In a few seconds, a message is delivered that leaves a life long impact to the individual hearing
as well as to those who the word is being delivered to.

Discerning the Human Spirit

Of all of the ones mentioned, discerning the human spirit will be the most controversial. Can any
really know what's in the heart of man? When Simon the sorcerer saw the apostles laying hands on people,
that they had received the Holy Spirit, he asked to purchase the gift of God. Look at Peter's response:

*"But Peter said to him, "May your silver perish with you, because you thought you could obtain the gif
God with money! You have no part or portion in this matter, for your heart is not right before God. The
fore repent of this wickedness of yours, and pray the Lord that, if possible, the intention of your heart n
be forgiven you. For I see that you are in the gall of bitterness and in the bondage of iniquity." Acts 8:20*

Take notice that Peter didn't rebuke the demon but discerned what was in Peter's heart. We also see Je
using the discerning of spirits when addressing Nathaniel in John:

*"When Jesus saw Nathanael approaching, he said of him, "Here truly is an Israelite in whom there is
deceit." "How do you know me?" Nathanael asked." John 1:47-48*

Notice Nathaniel's response, "how do you know me?" Jesus discerned what was in Nathaniel's heart, wh
in returned caused him to feel known by the Lord. We are often afraid of what someone would see if they look
into our heart. That's what I love about Jesus, He always has the ability to see the good that He has deposited in

scerning the Holy Spirit

This is my favorite use of the gift of discerning of spirits. We often forget that the Holy Spirit is spirit. The pture says:

"Then John gave this testimony: "I saw the Spirit come down from heaven as a dove and remain on him. And I myself did not know him, but the one who sent me to baptize with water told me, 'The man on whom you see the Spirit come down and remain is the one who will baptize with the Holy Spirit.'" John 1:32-33

It's important to note that a bird didn't fly out of heaven and land on Jesus. John saw the Spirit coming down m heaven as a dove. I believe John saw the Spirit descend in the spirit.

I love discerning what the Spirit is doing in my life, and in the lives of others. I have been in services where Spirit of God would manifest Himself in the room with healing, or prophecy. I have learned, and I am con-uing to learn, how to be sensitive to what the Spirit wants to do. This is part of the gift of discerning of Spirits. e of the best examples of someone moving in the discerning of the Holy Spirit, is in the life and ministry of thryn Kuhlman.

ower Gifts (Faith, Healing and Miracles)

ft of Faith

Love is the currency of heaven. Love energizes faith, and nothing happens in the Kingdom of God without h. Faith accesses the invisible realm around us. In scripture, there are three types of faith: the measure of h, the eternal virtue of faith, and the gift of faith.

The *Gift of Faith*, like the other gifts, is something that "comes upon us" or is manifested through us as the irit wills. In that sense, as believers, we have access to all of the gifts since we possess the Holy Spirit. There y be gifts that flow through us more consistently than others, but if a spirit filled believer was dropped into an ligenous tribe somewhere, because of the Holy Spirit, they would possess all that those people need for the gdom to be expanded.

The gift of faith is one that I have experienced often. This gift is connected to a *rhema* word from the Lord. e word from the Lord may not be something I hear audibly; it could come as a thought, but when declared eases the substance of faith to those who need to hear it.

"So faith comes from hearing, and hearing
by the word of Christ." Romans 10:17

Gift of Healing

I have seen the gift of healing flow in four primary ways:

1. Word of faith

2. Word of knowledge

3. Laying on of hands

4. Atmosphere

"But what does it say? "The word is near you, in your mouth and in your heart"—that is, the word of fa which we are preaching." Romans 10:8

In the 1940's and 50's there was a healing revival called 'The Voice of Healing'. Men like William Branha Gordon Lindsey, A.A. Allen, Jack Coe and Oral Roberts where the catalyst to this movement. William Branh was probably the most famous of the healing evangelists during this revival. He had an extremely accurate w of knowledge gift that led to notable healings. Branham couldn't read, but God taught him to read the bi however, because of his challenges in reading he wasn't the best teacher. So in the beginning of Branham's m istry, he would have F.F Bosworth (the author of *Christ the Healer*), teach morning sessions on receiving a keeping your healing. After attending a certain amount of his sessions, people would receive a card that allo them to take part in the night service with Branham. Branham believed that people needed to hear the word faith to believe God for their miracle.

I have attended meetings, and ministered to people after sharing God's word on healing, and people wo have already received a healing without the laying on of hands. By just hearing the living word, people receiv their miracle. This is true also of sharing testimonies. As we have talked about in an earlier chapter, the testimo of Jesus is the Spirit of prophecy. Sharing testimonies of the sick being healed will often increase faith in he to believe that God heals. "If God healed them, why would He not heal me?"

The word of knowledge for healing reveals the sickness, and then releases faith to receive the healing. T word of knowledge is a great tool in personal evangelism as well. This is frequently called power evangelism. T Lord will give a word of knowledge about a person's condition, raising their faith level to be healed, and th often 'born again' after having this encounter with God.

ying on of Hands

> *"They will lay hands on the sick, and they will recover."*
> *Mark 16:18*

Laying on of hands is the most common way we see people healed. In the healing ministry of Oral Roberts, would have people line up in prayer lines while he sat on a stool. People would pass in front of him, he would hands on them, pray the prayer of faith, and people would receive their healing.

> *"While the sun was setting, all those who had any who were sick with various diseases brought them to Him;*
> *and laying His hands on each one of them, He was healing them."* Luke 4:40

Imagine our Lord and savior personally laying hands on all of these sick people. The value that He had for cing His hands on, and touching them, when all that He had to do was say a word and they would have been iled. I personally believe the laying on of hands has power to bring healing to the heart as well as the physical ly. Those with leprosy weren't accustomed to being touched, but Jesus stretched His hands out and cleansed m.

racles

One of my favorite miracle stories, that I personally witnessed, was when my wife Erica and I were students YWAM (Youth with a Mission) in Kona, Hawaii. Heidi Baker, a missionary in Mozambique, Africa was our est speaker. She shared a story of God multiplying chocolate chip cookies. There was no way for her to know t my class was responsible for the snack that afternoon, and we were dishing up chocolate chip cookies. The der knew there was no way we had enough cookies to serve everyone since the attendance easily tripled en people caught wind that Heidi would be ministering. After hearing Heidi's testimony of God multiplying kies to reveal His goodness to the African children, my leader said that there was no way he wasn't going to iltiply our cookies. So as we passed out the cookies, we just kept passing them out, and passing them out. I rsonally ate three cookies, and they kept passing the cookies around.

This is an example of a miracle. Biblical miracles would be the multiplying of the fishes and loaves, the rting of the red sea, money in the fish's mouth and turning water into wine. I call miracles 'showing up' and owing off'. Of course healings and answered prayer are considered miracles, but for the sake of sticking to bib- al definitions, healings and miracles are in different categories. Some would call a healing someone growing imb, or metal melting inside a body; however, these are more creative miracles than healings.

"In every encounter that I have had, the common denominator is always the voice of God."

Reflection Questions

1. Why are the Gifts of the Spirit critical to an empowered life?

_____

_____

_____

_____

2. What are the three Gifts of the Prophet, according to 1 Corinthians 12:8-11, that are discussed in t
   lesson?

_____

_____

_____

_____

3. Did the breakdown of the Three Levels of Prophecy help you better understand the different functions
   the prophetic? How do the different levels of the Prophetic pertain to Character, Credibility and Fav

_____

_____

_____

_____

4. A person with a gift of discernment has to be careful to not become critical. What are some of the practical things you can do to keep your heart motivated out of love? (See Philippians 1:9-10.)

_____

_____

_____

_____

5. What are the four primary ways that the Gift of Healing flows? Were you familiar with all four, or were some of them new to you?

_____

_____

_____

_____

[NOTES]

Lesson 9
Hearing the Voice of God

"Here I am! I stand at the door and knock. If anyone hears my voice and opens the door, I will come in and eat with that person, and they with me." Revelation 3:20

It's important to understand the culture in which this passage is taking place. We are not talking about dinner at a fast food restaurant. In Jewish families today, as well as many other cultures, meals are long family events filled with laughter and conversation. Jesus is inviting us to a feast with Him. This scripture is used often in evangelism, and it works, but the context is actually written to believers who where in Ephesus. I love teaching this passage of scripture in the context of hearing God's voice. God knocks on the door of our hearts waiting for us to respond. The question is what does the knock of God sound like?

It can become easy to dismiss the fact that God speaks; especially if we have never experienced his voice in a supernatural way. There are times God may speak audibly, but it's very rare. Most people that I have asked, how they hear God's voice say that His voice is very subtle. This is also how I tend to experience hearing the voice of God most often. Later in the next lesson, we are going to look at the "louder" ways God speaks, such as angels, visions, dreams etc., but right now let's discuss the subtle, still, small voice of God.

Here's a story to illustrate a subtle way God has spoken to me in the past. Once while preaching in a conference in New Jersey, my ear felt very hot. I continued to preach thinking I was just hot, and kept drinking water. After I preached, a woman walked over to me and told me that she was having a hard time believing some of my God stories, but then she saw my ear burning bright red and heard the Lord speak to her, "I'm speaking through him." That was very encouraging to me. A few months later, I was speaking at a conference in Nashville, Tennessee, where a very reputable prophet had a word for me. He told me that I would be in services, and my right ear would get burning hot with the fire of God. This was to be a sign that the gift of faith had come upon me, and I was to release miracles.

There was no way for this prophet to know that I had already experienced this months prior in a meeting. I had never read any books on someone having a burning right ear that represented the gift of faith. There are no formulas to the way God speaks. I believe God speaks to each one of us in unique ways. This is the same way that every relationship has its own ways of communicating and showing love. We have all just read the fourteen ways God speaks, but what if there are more than fourteen ways? What if God can speak to us any way He chooses? The same God who never changes, also never performed one miracle the same way in the bible. This shouldn't discourage the reader, but encourage us that God desires a relationship with us; He desires to speak to us as a friend speaks to a friend.

As believers, we have to possess the revelation that God speaks to His children. The enemy will often sow seeds of unbelief by causing us to question, "Has God really spoken?" This is why it is critical to be a student of the word. The Lord's voice will not contradict His word, however not everything God speaks to us is in His word. For example, you may hear from the Lord, through a word of knowledge, to minister to someone at a local convenience store. You won't find that in the bible, but it's clear it is God's desire that we minister to people and that God sent us to minister.

What does God's voice sound like? It's important to note that God speaks the way we hear. To me God sounds like me, sometimes like my wife, and very often like the Fathers in my life. God will often speak the way we listen, and it is often a voice that is very familiar.

How often do we enter the Presence of the Lord with no agenda other than to minister to the Lord? In a time when the word of the Lord was rare, that's exactly what Samuel did. There are seasons in our lives when it feels like God is not speaking to us. It is in those seasons that learning to worship and rest in the Presence of the Lord, are a must.

"Samuel was lying down in the house of the Lord, where the ark of God was...."

Sometimes when we don't know what to pray, or when we simply want to be with Jesus, we hear His voice. As we rest in His Presence and soak in His presence, the Lord comes into that place with us. I like to put on instrumental music and lie down. I don't pray long prayers; I just speak simple phrases to the Lord, then wait and listen for His voice. Often during this time, I will see pictures in my mind (called visions), have floods of thoughts fill my mind, or have scriptures come to my heart. By spending time in the presence of the Lord, we learn to discern the ways God speaks to us.

A good reminder for me personally while ministering to people is found in Revelation 19:10, *"The testimony of Jesus is the Spirit of prophecy"*. When we speak a word in the name of Jesus, it means that we are speaking in the nature and character of Jesus. Jesus is the savior, redeemer, comforter, healer, life giver, Father, brother, friend and so much more. Since Jesus is the redeemer, prophecy must have a redemptive element to it. Before prophesying, ask yourself if the word reflects Jesus' testimony? Does it point people to the Father in relationship?

"Rightly representing the heart of God must be our highest aim."

The Lord may have us give words at times that are hard, but we must have the humility and love like Daniel the prophet had when he spoke to Nebuchadnezzar. Daniel 4:19 says, "My lord, if only the dream applied to those who hate you and its interpretation to your adversaries!" In the prophetic ministry, rightly representing the God of love must be our highest aim.

Reflection Questions

1. It is easy to dismiss the subtle voice of God. What are some of the things you can do to quiet yourself to listen? Are there areas in your life that have become too busy to hear His voice?

_____

_____

_____

_____

2. How can we know that what we are hearing is from God?

_____

_____

_____

_____

3. "The testimony of Jesus is the Spirit of Prophecy." What do we need to know about God and His nature, so that when we are prophesying, we are releasing the testimony of Jesus?

_____

_____

_____

_____

[NOTES]

_____
_____
_____
_____
_____
_____
_____
_____
_____
_____
_____
_____
_____
_____
_____
_____
_____
_____
_____
_____
_____
_____
_____
_____
_____
_____

Lesson 10
Ways God Speaks

There are pitfalls to hearing God's voice. One of them being the tendency to compare the way you may hear, to the way another hears the voice of God.

"Mount Sinai was wrapped in smoke because the Lord descended upon it in fire; its smoke ascended like the smoke of a furnace, and the whole mountain quaked violently. And it happened, as the blast of the ram's horn grew louder and louder, Moses spoke and God answered him with [a voice of] thunder." Exodus 19:18-19 AMP

Moses heard God's voice in the fire, the smoke and the mountain quaking. Contrast this scripture now from how Elijah heard the Lord in 1 Kings:

"So He said, "Go forth and stand on the mountain before the Lord." And behold, the Lord was passing by! And a great and strong wind was rending the mountains and breaking in pieces the rocks before the Lord; but the Lord was not in the wind. And after the wind an earthquake, but the Lord was not in the earthquake. 12 After the earthquake a fire, but the Lord was not in the fire; and after the fire a sound of a gentle blowing. 13 When Elijah heard it, he wrapped his face in his mantle and went out and stood in the entrance of the cave. And behold, a voice came to him and said, "What are you doing here, Elijah?" 1 Kings 19:11-13

When we compare these two scriptures we see that they have the exact same manifestations, but the way God spoke to Moses wasn't the way God spoke to Elijah. Moses heard God in an extremely demonstrative way, but Elijah heard only a gentle blowing of the wind. I have encountered a lot of people in my ministry who feel as though they don't hear the voice of God. After asking a few questions, it is always the same thing. They actually hear God clearly, except they hear God in their thoughts. God's voice sounds to them as if they are just thinking something. What's amazing about this is that these people think they are missing out because they don't hear God audibly. When the truth is that they are already walking in an intimacy with the Lord where He doesn't have to yell at them. He only has to whisper. The scripture declares we have the mind of Christ, and those who walk closely to Jesus know His thoughts. We have become His, and He has become ours. This is heaven's mandate!

Seers

We discussed in an earlier chapter how God can choose to speak to us through our spiritual eyes. These are called visions. There are those in the body of Christ that visions are the primary way they hear from God. These prophetic individuals are called seers in the bible.

> *"Formerly in Israel, if someone went to inquire of God, they would say, "Come, let us go to the seer," because the prophet of today used to be called a seer."* 1 Samuel 9:9

> *"As for the events of King David's reign, from beginning to end, they are written in the records of Samuel the seer, the records of Nathan the prophet and the records of Gad the seer"* 1 Chronicles 29:29

Take notice in the Chronicles passage that the scripture distinguishes between the prophet and the seer. Both are prophets, but the seer describes how these prophetic individuals receive revelation from the Lord. Seers hear the voice of God through their eyes. One of my favorite passages that pull the veil back on the life of a seer is found in 2 Kings.

> *"Alas, my master! What shall we do?" So he answered, "Do not fear, for those who are with us are more than those who are with them." Then Elisha prayed and said, "O Lord, I pray, open his eyes that he may see." And the Lord opened the servant's eyes and he saw; and behold, the mountain was full of horses and chariots of fire all around Elisha."* 2 Kings 6:15-17

I would love to retell this story the way I imagine it. I picture Elisha as an older man sitting on a rocking chair, blanket over his waist, and sipping on a cup of tea. His younger less experienced disciple looks out the window and starts pacing back and forth freaking out. Elisha calmly prays, "Lord open my servant's eyes to see what I see."

"Seeing in the spirit realm what the Father is doing, changes our earthly perspective to a heavenly perspective."

Bubbling Forth

Another Hebrew word meaning *'to prophesy'*, that reveals how revelation can come, is the word *'naba'*. *Naba* means to flow, spring, bubble up, pour forth, spout, or to utter. Those with a naba prophetic flow often pray in the spirit before prophesying. This is unlike a seer who has to wait in the presence of the Lord to focus their mind and heart on Jesus through worship or meditation. A seer will often have to prophesy slower as they receive a picture from the Lord, and interpret what they are seeing; whereas a naba prophecy is more of a bubbling forth.

I have operated in both the seer and the naba flow, but most frequently I function in the naba. When I prophesy, most of the time I have no word from the Lord until I start praying for an individual. This flow requires more faith in God's desire to speak to an individual, than it does the prophetic gift. Most people want God to tell them everything before they minister to the person being highlighted, but that's not the way it generally works in this kind of flow. Prophesying this way requires faith and risk.

This is a non-exhaustive list of *some* of the ways God speaks:

1. His Word

> *"For the word of God is living and active. Sharper than any double-edged sword, it penetrates even to dividing soul and spirit, joints and marrow; it judges the thoughts and attitudes of the heart."* Hebrews 4:12 NIV

God speaks through His word. Very early in my walk with the Lord, I earnestly pursued spiritual gifts without reading the word. I read every book on the supernatural I could get my hands on. One day while doing listening prayer, I saw a vision of a field, and then I saw a pipe with water flowing through it. The water stopped flowing, and the vision tilted on its side. I asked the Lord what He was showing me, and He said, "That's you. The water of my word is not flowing in you, and you are becoming out of balance with all spirit and no word." After this experience, I pursued a deeper knowledge of the word

There is nothing wrong with reading books and listening to podcasts, but this should only be a part of our spiritual diet, not the whole meal. Learning to meditate upon the word, as well as understand the context of scripture, is critical. When I am reading the word, I will choose a book of the bible to study, and read the entire book. After that, I will go back to topics that where highlighted to me. I will make sure to get a clear understanding of the context of the verse by studying the chapter before and after. Taking scripture out of its original context creates error. It's important to note that no scripture is for private interpretation.

"The word of God is the sure word of prophecy."

2. Still Small Voice

> *"The LORD said, "Go out and stand on the mountain in the presence of the LORD, for the LORD is about to pass by." Then a great and powerful wind tore the mountains apart and shattered the rocks before the LORD, but the LORD was not in the wind. After the wind there was an earthquake, but the LORD was not in the earthquake. After the earthquake came a fire, but the LORD was not in the fire. And after the fire came a gentle whisper."* I Kings 19:11-12 NIV

The still small voice can also come like a flood of thoughts. One way to practice hearing the still small voice of God is through journaling. Habakkuk was told to "write the vision". I have had many students in bible schools that I have taught, struggle with hearing God's voice. One common denominator was that they all had analytical personalities. They would think they heard God and then begin to question, "Was that me or was that God?"

I'm the opposite. I'm more of a creative and visual person. I could be driving in the car thinking about nothing and hear, "Son, stay home today." It wouldn't be something I was thinking about, or asking the Lord. The last time this happened to me, my boys had a special event at school that I would have missed if I hadn't stayed home, and not taken any appointments. It was important to God that I spent time with my boys.

3. Dreams

"For God does speak now one way, now another though man may not perceive it. In a dream, in a vision of the night, when deep sleep falls on men as they slumber in their beds…" Job 33:14

Dreams are a very common way for believers and unbelievers to hear the Lord. The Lord will often give dreams to the unbeliever to draw them to himself. Joseph interpreted Pharaoh's dream, and we are in a season where God is raising up Joseph's and Daniel's; those who will interpret the dreams of the Pharaohs of our day.

How do we know if a dream is from God? Dreams from God often leave us hungry for an interpretation. They will often come up in random times of the day. "Ah, I just remembered that I had a dream." There are dreams that are literal, but most dreams are parabolic in nature, filled with symbols.

4. Visions.

"It will come about after this That I will pour out My Spirit on all mankind; and your sons and daughters will prophesy, your old men will dream dreams, your young men will see visions." Joel 2:28

Visions are often referred to as mental pictures. Visions can take place internally, externally, as well as with eyes open or closed. We can't make vision's happen by willing them. I have experienced visions most often times when praying for people. The word 'vision' throws people off, when learning how to hear God's voice, because they are expecting a massive television screen to open up before them. When I share with people how I see a vision, people often exhale and say, "I've had those since I was a kid." As I pray for people a picture may pop up in my mind. I have learned to pay attention to them. I will quietly ask the Holy Spirit what He is showing me.

God will use our imaginations to speak to us. The new age calls this the third eye or mind's eye, but the bible calls this (in Ephesians), the eyes of our heart. Many people hear God's voice with their eyes.

5. Voice of the Lord

There are two ways we can hear the voice of the Lord. The *inner audible* voice, which many have described to sound like thunder coming from the inside, and then there is the *audible* voice of the Lord.

I have had experiences with both the inner and audible voice of the Lord. The day I was pulled away from a bullet as an innocent bystander in a drive by shooting, I heard an inner audible voice, like a very loud thought, "Where would you go if you died right now?" I'm still amazed, and theologically confused, at how God could speak on the inside of me when I wasn't yet born again.

My encounter with the audible voice of the Lord happened months after I got born again. I loved Jesus, and felt very near to Him, but church was hard for me. I was one of the youngest guys in the church, and I went alone. I had lost all of my friends after I had gotten saved, because I stopped living the party life style. It didn't take long until I started to fall back into my old ways, and fall back into compromise. One night I was feeling tormented demonically. I had never experienced such fear. I could see something moving in my room, but it wasn't human. I curled up and wept not knowing what to do. I heard quietly in my spirit, "The blood of Jesus!" repeatedly. So I began to cry out, "The blood of Jesus! The blood of Jesus!" I began to feel a wind blow over me, and then heard audibly in my ear, "Ivan." Instantly peace came over me, and I fell asleep. When I woke up I heard my name again, but this time not in the outside of my heart, but on the inside of my heart.

The next morning when I woke up, I began to process the voice that I had heard. It was a very emotional moment for me. If my mother would have walked in my room during this moment, she would have turned the light on and asked me how I was doing because of how hard I was weeping. I knew the voice I heard wasn't the voice of my own father, because my father has a very deep voice, and I would have known if it was him. This voice was different. Then it hit me. It was God who spoke to me. This moved my heart greatly. I ran into the bathroom, and put the shower on so that my mother wouldn't hear me crying. Then a thought came into my mind, "If God spoke to me, why didn't He give me some secret message?" Then I heard as clear as day, but in my thoughts, "I'm calling you. Whenever you are ready to follow me, I'm calling you."

6. Trances

Trances are a state that God brings us into, often followed by a vision.

"I was in the city of Joppa praying, and in a trance I saw a vision. I saw something like a large sheet being let down from heaven by its four corners, and it came down to where I was." Acts 11:5 NIV

In many of Mariah Woodworth Etter's meetings in the early 1900's, trances were a very common manifestation. Young and old would fall into a *trance like* state, very often seeing heaven and hell. Her ministry was controversial in her day for the signs and wonders, but mostly because of the trances. One story I read was about a skeptic journalist who came to disprove the phony claims of the trance evangelist. This man personally fell into a trance, and after his experience, documented having seen heaven and hell. The experience caused him to give his life to Christ.

7.   Angels

"In speaking of the angels he says, "He makes his angels winds, his servants flames of fire." Hebrews 1:7 NIV

There are many different types of angels in the scripture, but two primary angels that are mentioned in scripture are Gabriel, a Messenger Angel and Michael (the Archangel), a Warrior Angel. The Messenger Angel brings messages, while the Warrior Angel brings protection. The job of these angels, often times, is to bring people to Christ.

"Are they not all ministering spirits, sent out to render service for the sake of those who will inherit salvation?" Hebrews 1:14

There are also beliefs that each one of us has a guardian angel.

"See that you do not despise one of these little ones, for I say to you that their angels in heaven continually see the face of My Father who is in heaven." Matthew 18:10

One day my wife was out running errands, and her car broke down on the side of the road. Where she broke down happened to be a very hilly area of Oregon where we lived at the time. She was forced to begin pushing the vehicle by herself up a hill. Then suddenly, from out of nowhere, a man appeared, and began pushing the vehicle for her. After the car had been pushed out of the way, she looked back to thank the man, but he was gone. This could have been a coincidence, but I didn't believe so and neither did she.

Reflection Questions

1.   Why is it so important that we do not compare ourselves to how others hear the voice of God?

_____

_____

_____

_____

2. How do we know if a dream is from God? (See Isaiah 29:8)

_____

_____

_____

_____

3. What are some of the ways that God has spoken to you? Ask the Lord to speak to you in a new way.

_____

_____

_____

_____

[NOTES]

[Section Four]
Flowing in the Prophetic

Lesson 11
Prophetic Types

As we grow in understanding in the prophetic call, it is imperative to understand the diversity of this office. As unique as each individual's personality can be, that is how diverse the prophetic can be. No two prophets function the same way. In scripture, the word 'prophet' is attached to men like Abraham, Moses, Elijah, Elisha and Ezekiel, to name a few. Each prophet mentioned receives revelation from God differently, and then delivers the word of the Lord differently.

Abraham - The Friend of God Prophet.

The first person in the bible to be called a prophet was Abraham. In Genesis 20:6-7, a heathen prince had taken Abraham's wife. God then commanded the king to restore Abraham's wife to him, saying of Abraham, "He is a prophet!" There are no recorded prophecies that Abraham declared. Abraham establishes, however, the foundation of all prophets, friendship with God.

> *"The foundation of all prophets should be friendship with God."*

James 2:23 says that the scripture was fulfilled when, *"Abraham believed God, and it was reckoned to him as righteousness,"* and he was called a friend of God. Abraham is an example of a prophet who obeyed out of a place of trust and friendship with God. Hearing, obeying and even "wrestling" with God in prayer is an attribute we'll find in almost all of the prophets. Prophets should first be God's friends.

There are different levels of friendship:

1. Acquaintance (superficial level):

This is the level where the conversation revolves around the weather or news. Nothing deep here.

2. Getting to know one another:

This is where the conversation moves on to personal interest, pushing past the superficial level. In this level we discover interests and passions.

3. The Confidante:

This is the level where you can entrust the secrets of your heart.

4. Covenant Friendship:

This is the level of relationship God desires for His people to walk in. This level is established most often in marriage.

Friendships are built over time, through vulnerability and exposing our hearts to one another. This requires both quality time and quantity of time. The same is true with cultivating friendship with God. We give Him our hearts, we let Him see and know the deeper secrets within us, and we spend quality and quantity of time in His presence. It is out of this place we learn to recognize His voice.

A true prophetic person longs to have a hearing heart. So our hearts need to always be in a position to hear the Father's voice. I do this constantly when I'm talking to someone who wants counsel. I will listen with my ears, but I will also listen with my heart to hear what the Father is saying to that person.

Moses - Governmental, Signs and Wonders Prophet

"Since that time no prophet has risen in Israel like Moses, whom the Lord knew face to face, for all the signs and wonders which the Lord sent him to perform in the land of Egypt against Pharaoh, all his servants, and all his land, and for all the mighty power and for all the great terror which Moses performed in the sight of all Israel." Deuteronomy 34:10-12

The passion to hear the voice of God is found in the life of all the prophets, but how they function, and even hear the Lord, is different. Moses had one of the deepest relationships with God. His intimacy with God is more than any other prophet in scripture, other than Jesus Himself.

"Hear now My words: if there is a prophet among you, I, the Lord, shall make Myself known to him in a vision. I shall speak with him in a dream."Not so, with My servant Moses, he is faithful in all My house-hold; with him I speak mouth to mouth, even openly, and not in dark sayings, and he beholds the form of the Lord. Why then were you not afraid to speak against My servant, against Moses?" Numbers 12:6-8

Moses didn't only have visions and dreams, he also beheld the form of the Lord. In another passage of scripture it says, *"Moses spoke to God face to face"* (Ex 33:11). When the scripture says 'seek God's face', the word in Hebrew is 'paneem', which is the same word for 'presence'. Moses was a lover of the Presence of God, and all forms that God spoke. As a prophetic people, hungering for God's presence should be the utmost priority of our lives.

What makes Moses different than other prophets in scripture? Well other than Elijah and Elisha, Moses is one of the few prophets that had signs and wonders following him.

Signs and wonders were understood in Moses' day as a sign that God was with the person performing them. The supernatural was commonplace in the regions of Moses' day, as was also proven by Pharaoh's magicians, as they were able to reproduce most of Moses' signs.

Moses operated in many different ways as a prophet. He not only moved in the power of God, but he also led a nation. While Moses was on Mt. Sinai for 40 days, he was shown how to build the tabernacle. He was given by God the lay out, and specific measurements of the tabernacle. Today, in the body of Christ, there are prophets that function this way. The Lord will show them the blue prints of what they are to build on the earth

Prophets help to lay a foundation by seeing God's blue prints for a church, or whatever sphere they serve in. Prophetic leaders are also given structures, or what we now call 'wineskins', for movements. Some would say that this is the work of an apostle, but the blueprints are generally given to a prophet, while the apostle is the one who lays the foundation.

Moses started off his ministry like many leaders do, meeting with every person that had need, which ultimately leads to burn out.

Elijah and Elisha – The Demonstration Prophet

Elijah is known as the prophet of the Lord that moved in incredible power. In Elijah's lifetime, he was used by God to resurrected the widow's son; he called fire from heaven; he started a drought; he then prophesied and caused it to rain by the power of prayer, and that only names a few of the miracles recorded of Elijah. There are prophets today that move in signs and wonders. Elisha saw a double portion of the miracles that Elijah saw.

Demonstration Prophets are also known as Signs Prophets. They are known as such because God displays signs and wonders to confirm the prophetic word that was delivered. I have met prophets that function in this realm. One such prophet is a mentor of mine, Bobby Conner. At a meeting a friend of mine attended, he testified that Bobby was preaching about the power of God, and the need for the church to lay a hold of it. Bobby then pointed at the lights in the stadium he was preaching in, and they started to explode. Every light he pointed to exploded. This was a sign God supernaturally brought to emphasize the teaching Bobby was bringing, that the church needed to lay ahold of God's power.

The Signs Prophet are not just known by demonstration, but also the life of the prophet can be the prophetic sign. A few biblical examples of this would be the life of Hosea, and the life of Ezekiel.

Samuel and Habakkuk – The Seer Prophet

We have already seen, earlier in this book, the breakdown of how a seer gift functions; however, here we want to look at the function and purpose of the Seer Prophet.

I believe the call of a Seer Prophet, is to reveal the supernatural to the body of Christ. Samuel and Habakkuk are two prophets that I believe exemplify this.

Samuel had one of the most accurate word of knowledge gifts found in scripture, second to Christ. In 1 Samuel 9, by the word of knowledge, Samuel gives Saul details about his life, and what Saul was about to encounter, more than any other place found in scripture. The gifts of the seer prophet are: word of knowledge, word of wisdom and discerning of spirits. The discerning of spirits gift is the ability to see in the spirit.

Habakkuk gives insight into how the Seer Prophet's gift functions:

"I will stand my watch and set myself on the rampart, and watch to see what He will say to me, and what I will answer when I am corrected. Then the Lord answered me and said: "Write the vision and make it plain on tablets, that he may run who reads it. For the vision is yet for an appointed time; but at the end it will speak, and it will not lie. Though it tarries, wait for it; because it will surely come, it will not tarry."
Habakkuk 2:1-3 (NKJV)

Take notice what Habakkuk says,*" I will watch to see what He will say to me."*

Habakkuk heard God's voice through his spiritual eyes. Seer Prophets often have visions, dreams, trances and angelic encounters. Through the sharing of the accurate revelation from God to the individuals, church, region or nation, the seer prophets reveals the closeness of heaven to us.

There are many more types of prophets we can find in scripture, as well as functioning on the earth today. This is not a comprehensive list, but a few types of prophets that have not already been mentioned that I am aware of, are as follows:

1. Writing Prophets

Rick Joyner would be a modern day writing prophet. He has seer type encounters with God that he publishes in books, and prophetic journals. Final Quest is a book by Joyner that warns, predicts and guides the body of Christ

2. Prophetic Evangelist

These types of evangelists carry the heart of God for the lost. They are constantly prophesying of the harvest, and the need for the church to focus on the lost. Patricia King is a great example of a prophetic evangelist. She walks in the function of prophet, but one of the main focuses of her ministry is the lost.

3. Prophetic Teachers

Prophetic Teachers are equippers. They love to teach and train the body to hear the voice of God, and they break up the scriptures into small chunks of bread that the people can digest. The messages they teach are messages that always carry a prophetic edge. James Goll is a great example of a prophetic teacher. He expounds on scripture like many other teachers, but carries an anointing like the *Sons of Issachar,* to know times and seasons.

This gift allows the prophet to teach the word in a manner that brings the scripture alive to what the Father is saying in the current hour.

4. Prophetic Intercessors

These intercessors are carriers of God's heart for justice. They see the injustices in our land, and can literally feel God's heart breaking over them. Prophetic intercessors become God's trumpets over areas of injustice. A modern example of a prophetic intercessor would be Lou Engle. He has gathered the body of Christ in several strategic assemblies, named *The Call*, too fast and pray for our nation.

5. Prophetic Preaching

Prophetic Preachers, different than teachers, often don't know what they are going to preach until they grab ahold of the microphone. They often start their messages by saying, "I planned a totally different message, and God changed it." These preachers become the voice of God when they are preaching. Mike Bickle would be a modern example of a prophetic preacher.

False Prophets

Many places in scripture we are warned to *beware* of False Prophets. What makes a prophet a false one? I think it's important to distinguish the difference between a False Prophets, and someone who is a wrong prophet. In the New Testament, we are encouraged to practice hearing God's voice and to exercise our gifts, especially prophecy. Missing a word doesn't make the person giving the word a False Prophet.

"But the prophet who presumes to speak a word in My name, which I have not commanded him to speak, or who speaks in the name of other gods, that prophet shall die.' And if you say in your heart, 'How shall we know the word which the Lord has not spoken?'— when a prophet speaks in the name of the Lord, if the thing does not happen or come to pass, that is the thing which the Lord has not spoken; the prophet has spoken it presumptuously; you shall not be afraid of him." Deuteronomy 18:20-22

There is a lot loaded into this verse, but the first thing I want to point out is that a prophet can miss a word because they are operating out of presumption, and we are told to not be afraid of them. A False Prophet, however, is someone who is a wolf in sheep's clothing. Their prophecy is purposefully trying to steer people away from the Lord to another god. What determines a False Prophet can be broken down into these four categories:

1. Different Source. (1 John 4:1)

Today there are psychics, mediums and other spiritualists that prophesy. Their source is not the Holy Spirit This is why the scripture tells us to test the spirits.

2. Different Message. (Galatians 1:8-9)

There are many cults in the world that seem to have a Christian foundation, but their message is not the same as the gospels.

3.   Different Fruit. (Matthew 7:16-18)

What is the fruit of the prophet's life? Every person has clay feet, but if the prophet's life is leading people towards a path of destruction, this is a good indicator that the messenger should not be trusted.

4.   Different End. (Proverbs 14:12)

There's an old saying, "You're headed where you're going." There are many tragic stories of False Prophets forming cults that ultimately led to lives being destroyed in the end.

By reviewing the four characteristics of false prophets, we can see modern examples of False Prophets that have led false movements. Movements such as The Church of Jesus Christ of Latter Day Saints and The Jehovah's Witness. Both of these cults do not appropriately recognize the deity of Christ. Mormons believe Jesus is the brother of Satan, and Jehovah's Witnesses believe Jesus was Jehovah's first creation. These are only one of the many false teachings in these cults; however, challenging the deity of Christ is heresy. .

All of this is evidence that it is important to learn to love the word of God, be a part of a healthy church community, and allow people to speak into our lives to ensure we will be kept on the straight and narrow. I have personally chosen to glean from teachers from many different streams in the body of Christ. Every facet of the body of Christ carries a truth that we all need to be strengthened. It's important that we don't begin to accuse our own brothers and sisters in Christ of being False Prophets, simply because we differ on certain doctrine. What is important is that we recognize what the major foundational truths are in scripture, and agree on those.

How Do I know if I'm a Prophet?

Is someone born a prophet? Can I fast and pray to become a prophet? Ultimately how do I know if I'm called to be a prophet?

I have not only heard these questions, but also personally asked these questions. I don't believe having a title is important, what is important is function. By studying the lives of prophets in scripture, you'll find that some like Jeremiah were called to be prophets when still in their mother's womb. Others like Amos were called later in life.

"The bottom line is, the calling of prophet is not a self-appointed one.
It is one that is called by God, and recognized by people."

A great example of what I am talking about is found in the life of David. When David was just a boy, the Lord had called him to be King. God chose David, but used Samuel to anoint him King. Yet still David had to grow up in his calling, and his calling became visible to the people he was called to lead.

The scripture says of both Samuel and Jesus that they "grew in favor and stature with God and man." Someone may be called to be a prophet, but I like to picture it as a child wearing his or her parent's clothing, they still have a lot of growing to do. If Jesus had to grow in favor and stature, then to me that means that we all must grow in favor and stature.

We are all called to prophesy, as we have been learning, but we are not all called to be prophets. Prophet is a function given to the body of Christ to equip the saints to hear the voice of God, as well as to speak forth the mind and counsel of God to the people.

> *"More than a title, or gift, our motivation must be love.*
> *If we choose love we will never fail."*

Reflection Questions

1. There are five different levels of friendship that we talked about in this lesson. How is this important in our relationship with God as a prophetic minister?

    _____

    _____

    _____

    _____

2. How do we see the function of a signs and wonders prophet in the church today?

    _____

    _____

    _____

    _____

3. Why is it important that we know the difference between a False Prophet and a Wrong Prophet?

_____

_____

_____

_____

4. How do you know if you are a prophet?

_____

_____

_____

_____

[NOTES]

Lesson 12
Practical Keys to Flowing in Prophetic Revelation

Presence of God

"Do you not know that you are a temple of God and that the Spirit of God dwells in you?" 1 Corinthians 3:16

The revelation that the Holy Spirit abides within us will cause us to learn to listen with the ears of our hearts; turning inward to hear the voice of the Lord. Very often what I have witnessed when training people in the prophetic is that people are waiting to hear a booming voice audible in their ears; however, when they begin to learn to quiet themselves, and tune their hearts toward the indwelling of the Holy Spirit, they begin to hear clearly the whispers of God.

Fellowship or communion with the Holy Spirit is critical in growing in intimacy with the Lord, as well as the growing ability to hear His voice. Most believers have never considered talking to the Holy Spirit, but we have to understand that He is God on the earth since the Father and Son are seated, enthroned in heaven.

Learning to enter into the Presence of the Lord, through faith and communion with the Holy Spirit, is the first key in flowing in the prophetic anointing.

Rest

The second key is learning to rest in the Presence of the Lord. It is out of rest that revelation flows. I have often seen people who testify of not being able to hear God, but after observing the situation, I see that they are striving to hear His voice. I heard a revelation years ago, that I loved. It was the covenant name of God, Yahweh. According to Rabbinic tradition, when God spoke His name to Moses, He breathed it. I grew up with asthma, and know what it's like to struggle to breathe. As a boy, I would lose at hide and seek every time I played, because all my friends knew that all they needed to do was stay quiet for a moment, and they would hear me wheezing. Many in the church are wheezing, spiritually speaking, because they are striving so hard to please God. The scripture declares, *"In Him we live and move and have our being."* Life in Christ should be like breathing. It is out of this place of resting in God that revelation flows.

It is interesting to note that Adam's first day alive was the day God rested. One of Adam's first revelations of God would have been that He rested. Also in the book of Genesis, we find that the day started in the evening. So in the Hebrew culture, when the sun would set, that would be the start of a new day. Every day would be started with sleep. Rest reveals a very important aspect of the nature of God. Here's a great verse revealing this truth:

"Then Moses said to the Lord, "See, You say to me, 'Bring up this people!' But You Yourself have not let me know whom You will send with me. Moreover, You have said, 'I have known you by name, and you have also found favor in My sight.' Now therefore, I pray You, if I have found favor in Your sight, let me know Your ways that I may know You, so that I may find favor in Your sight. Consider too, that this nation is Your people." And He said, "My presence shall go with you, and I will give you rest." Exodus 33:12-14

Moses asked the Lord two questions:

1. Who will You send with me?

2. Show me Your ways that I may know You?

The Lord responds in verse 14, *"My Presence shall go with you, and I will give you rest."* This revelation is found in many other places in scripture. Christ Himself declares this in Matthew:

"Are you tired? Worn out? Burned out on religion? Come to me. Get away with me and you'll recover your life. I'll show you how to take a real rest. Walk with me and work with me—watch how I do it. Learn the un-forced rhythms of grace. I won't lay anything heavy or ill-fitting on you. Keep company with me and you'll learn to live freely and lightly." Matthew 11:28-30 (MSG)

Jesus is the answer to the rest we all need. He is the Lord of the Sabbath. Rest is no longer just one day off, even though that is important. Rest is found in learning to abide in Him.

Compelled by Love

"For Christ's love compels us." 2 Corinthians 5:14

When the goal of our ministry is to show someone the love of God, we will never go wrong. I have missed words of knowledge in the market place before, but because my heart was to show love to the person, they were still able to encounter the Father. My faith doesn't rest on my gifting, but my faith rests on knowing God's thoughts towards His people are as numerous as the sands on the seashore. God's thoughts towards His people are filled with love. I have confidence, when ministering over people, that the Lord always has an encouraging word for His children.

Faith and Risk

The fourth key is found in Galatians 5:6, *"Faith works through love."* Another way of saying this is, "love energizes our faith". This is one of the hardest steps, simply because stepping out in faith is taking a risk. I have met many individuals who have studied the prophetic ministry, received prayers of impartation, but have never applied the teachings. They find themselves still struggling to feel as though they have a gift of prophecy. On the other hand, I have met individuals that think, after one teaching on the prophetic, they can prophesy over everything that walks. These people may not have all the scripture, but they have the faith to apply what they have learned.

Be Yourself

The fifth and final is key is to simply be yourself. I've been in churches where the person delivering a prophetic word first shouts out in tongues, then proceeds to speak in King James English, all the while shaking violently. This type of ministry may flow well in certain gatherings, but delivering a word like this at the office may scare a person away. Learning to be supernaturally 'natural' is a huge key in the anointing flowing without hindrance.

Study the way your gift operates. For some it's through art, song or even writing an encouraging note to someone. It's important that even though you permit the Holy Spirit to stretch your faith, that we are true to who God has called us to be. I have seen comparison shut down more people's gifts than unbelief. Learning to be comfortable in your own skin is critical to flowing at highest capacity.

Reflection Questions

1. What are some of the ways we can learn to enter into communion with the Holy Spirit?

_____

_____

_____

_____

2. Out of rest revelation flows. What are some practical ways that you can be more intentional about being a person that encounters the rest that God brings?

_____

_____

_____

_____

3. We should all have the freedom to be ourselves. Comparison shuts down more peoples gifting than unbelief. Take some time to ask the Lord if there are areas where you have allowed comparison or the fear of man to hinder you from being yourself. Then ask the Holy Spirit to come into those areas and bring freedom.

_____

_____

_____

_____

[NOTES]

[Section Five]
Supernatural Realm

Lesson 13
Open Heavens

Many in the church have been praying the prayer out of Isaiah 64, *"Oh that you would rend the heavens and come down"*. The heart behind this prayer is beautiful. The prayer is a petition to have the manifest presence of God with us. The reality is, however, that Jesus already has rent the heavens and has come down. So much so, that the veil, in the holy of holies, was torn from top to bottom, making a place for us to have direct access to the Presence of Father God. If that's not enough, the scripture teaches us that we have been raised up with Christ and are seated with Him in heavenly places. (Eph 2:6) The statement that, "We can have as much of God as we want." is true. Some have taught, out of the book of Deuteronomy, that the heavens are closed because of the curse, and that we are given keys to open the heavens. This is naive at best, and at worst, it is a complete misunderstanding of what Christ has accomplished for His people on the cross.

I am an open heaven! Does that sound arrogant? Well, I am a child of God, and so are you. When we understand the position we have in Christ, and all that He has accomplished for us, it will create a supernatural ministry out of rest with no striving.

In Genesis 28, Jacob had a dream that greatly impacted him:

"Then Jacob departed from Beersheba and went toward Haran. He came to a certain place and spent the night there, because the sun had set; and he took one of the stones of the place and put it under his head, and lay down in that place. He had a dream, and behold, a ladder was set on the earth with its top reaching to heaven; and behold, the angels of God were ascending and descending on it." Genesis 28:10-12

"Then Jacob awoke from his sleep and said, "Surely the Lord is in this place, and I did not know it." He was afraid and said, "How awesome is this place! This is none other than the house of God, and this is the gate of heaven." Genesis 28:16-17

The mindset of the people, in Jacob's day, was that their 'gods' were regional. So, for Jacob to encounter God in another region made him think, "This must be God's house." A few chapters later, Jacob realizes the full revelation at Bethel.

"Then God said to Jacob, "Arise, go up to Bethel and live there..." Genesis 35:1

And then....

"So Jacob came to Luz (that is, Bethel), which is in the land of Canaan, he and all the people who were

with him. He built an altar there, and called the place El-bethel, because there God had revealed Himself to him when he fled from his brother." Genesis 35:6-7

Jacob starts with the revelation that God's house is in one geographical location, because that was where he had the dream of the heavens being open. Later when Jacob was instructed to go back to that place, he changes the name from Bethel (meaning house of God), to El Bethel (which means the God of the house of God). You see Jacob realizing, throughout his journey, that God didn't just camp out at Bethel, but was everywhere Jacob was.

"God is not far from you."

Let's look at John 1 to expound being an open heaven:

"Jesus replied, "Because I said to you that I saw you under the fig tree, do you believe [in Me]? You will see greater things than this." Then He said to him, "I assure you and most solemnly say to you, you will see heaven opened and the angels of God ascending and descending on the Son of Man [the bridge between heaven and earth]."John 1:50-51 AMP

Jesus is quoting Jacob, saying that He is the fulfillment of Jacob's ladder. The only way to the Father is through the Son, and Jesus is the bridge between heaven and earth (as the amplified puts it). As children of God, we have the Spirit of God living in us the same way the angels of God ascended and descended upon Jesus. Just as Jesus is the only way to the Father, the angels ascend and descend over us because we are the gate way for people to meet Christ.

Let's look at one other scripture to solidify this point:

"Now when all the people were baptized, Jesus was also baptized, and while He was praying, heaven was opened, and the Holy Spirit descended upon Him in bodily form like a dove, and a voice came out of heaven, "You are My beloved Son, in You I am well-pleased." Luke 3:21-22

As the heavens were opened over Jesus, they were opened over all of us. There's no place in scripture that says the heavens closed back up. We walk under an open heaven with direct access to the presence of God surrounded by angels. With this revelation, the understanding of the spiritual realm should open up to us.

Understanding that heaven isn't far from us, but is actually within reach, should create confidence in our ability to hear the voice of God, and to encounter the realm where God abides.

Reflection Questions

1. Why is it important, as a child of God, to have an understanding that we are an open heaven?

_____

_____

_____

_____

2. Knowing that heaven is actually within our reach, how does that affect your confidence level to hear God's voice? Have you struggled with feeling like heaven was far from you?

_____

_____

_____

_____

3. Practice being an open heaven. Go to a public place, like a coffee shop, and quietly worship and meditate upon the word. Then begin to pray for the glory of the Lord to touch those people around you. Be open to people coming up and asking you questions about Jesus.

_____

_____

_____

_____

[NOTES]

_____
_____
_____
_____
_____
_____
_____
_____
_____
_____
_____
_____
_____
_____
_____
_____
_____
_____
_____
_____
_____
_____
_____
_____
_____
_____
_____

Lesson 14
Encountering God

The scripture declares, *"All have sinned and fallen short of the glory of God"*. This verse has been used continually to remind God's people they are sinners saved by grace; however, the next verse is critical in understanding the full context of what was being said:

"Being justified as a gift by His grace through the redemption, which is in Christ Jesus;" Romans 3:24

Let's look at the same verse in the NLT for greater clarity:

"Yet God freely and graciously declares that we are righteous. He did this through Christ Jesus when he freed us from the penalty for our sins." Romans 3:24 NLT

Jesus took our sins upon on the cross making us the righteousness of God. The question for a Christian in the new covenant is, "Are you a sinner saved by grace, or a son being led into glory?

"For it was fitting for Him, for whom are all things, and through whom are all things, in bringing many sons to glory." Hebrews 2:10

Some may answer that both are true, but this thinking leads to dualism. This is the view that we are constantly in a fight to kill our old man, or old self. The scriptures teach that the old man has 'been' (past tense) crucified in Christ and we live by faith in the Son of God. (Gal 2:20) We are Sons and daughters who are meant to encounter our father. God is our Father, and His desire is that His sons and daughters hear His voice, as well as experience His Presence.

"We are sons and daughters who are meant to encounter our Father."

"[That you may really come] to know [practically, through experience for yourselves] the love of Christ, which far surpasses mere knowledge [without experience]; that you may be filled [through all your being] unto all the fullness of God [may have the richest measure of the divine Presence, and become a body wholly filled and flooded with God Himself]!" Ephesians 3:19 AMP

Experiencing God is not only biblical, it is critical if we are to be changed into His image. We also need this experience if we are to be a vessel in which others are to encounter God.

Jesus said to the Pharisees in John 5:

"You search the Scriptures because you think they give you eternal life. But the Scriptures point to me! Yet you refuse to come to me to receive this life." John 5:39-40 NLT

The word of God should lead us to God Himself. It is God's desire that we come to truly know Him.

When God chooses to reveal Himself to us, any encounters we may have through His word in worship, prayer, dream or any of the forms we have discussed, makes the word come alive. It's no longer words written on the pages of some ancient manuscript, but a word that has been written on our hearts.

Moses had so much glory on His face that He had to wear a veil on His face. The scripture tells us that we are *not* to put a veil on our faces, but actually that the veil has been lifted when people turn to Christ. We are called to walk in the light of God's glory.

"Therefore having such a hope, we use great boldness in our speech, and are not like Moses, who used to put a veil over his face so that the sons of Israel would not look intently at the end of what was fading away. But their minds were hardened; for until this very day at the reading of the old covenant the same veil remains unlifted, because it is removed in Christ. But to this day whenever Moses is read, a veil lies over their heart; but whenever a person turns to the Lord, the veil is taken away. Now the Lord is the Spirit, and where the Spirit of the Lord is, there is liberty. But we all, with unveiled face, beholding as in a mirror the glory of the Lord, are being transformed into the same image from glory to glory, just as from the Lord, the Spirit." 2 Corinthians 3:12-18

We are transformed from glory to glory by the principle of beholding and becoming. When we behold the Lord in His word, we are being transformed to be like Him. It is those who have encountered God that shake cities and change nations.

"World changers encounter God."

"Jesus answered him, "I assure you and most solemnly say to you, unless a person is born again [reborn from above—spiritually transformed, renewed, sanctified], he cannot [ever] see and experience the kingdom of God." John 3:3 AMP

There is a difference between entering the kingdom and seeing the kingdom. The day we take our last breath, we will enter into God's kingdom for all eternity. Seeing the kingdom means to experience God's kingdom on this side of eternity.

It may be hard to believe that people today are having supernatural encounters with God like those in this manual. A huge part of that is simply because we haven't been taught that, as believers, we are supernatural.

As new creations in Christ we are Spirit, we have a soul and live in a body. Hearing God's voice, and sensing His presence, is all taking place within our spirit man. We have lived in fallen conditions for so long, that we haven't learned to listen with our born again spirits.

The Hebrew mindset had a place for encounters with God. The culture was oratory, and they passed stories down from one generation to another. The Hebrews passed down stories of their grandfather Moses encountering God in a burning bush, or how their Great grandfather Abraham fed three men (two angels and the Lord Himself). (Gen 18:8) For a Hebrew boy growing up in the Far East, supernatural encounters were a part of their worldview. We struggle because our worldview is based more on the Greco-Roman worldview which emphasizes reason and analytical thinking. It is with the heart one believes unto righteousness, not the mind (Romans 10:10).

A renewed mind isn't struggling with unbelief over miracles, healings, and angelic encounters. We are all growing in our faith, and I have personally found that people who receive the most miracles are the ones that need them the most. As we encounter God, and the breakthroughs come, the miracles become an expectation because we grow in our understanding of the ways of God. When was the last time you were in a position where you needed a word from God, or a miracle for a loved one? It's often people in these positions that have the greatest testimonies..

While most of us long to walk with God in the garden like Adam did before the fall, the reality is that in our 'new creation reality', we have a greater reality than Adam. Adam walked with God, but God lives in us. It may take all of our years, on this side of eternity, learning to walk with God, hear His voice, bask in His presence and release His heart on the earth; but it's definitely something worth pursuing.

Reflection Questions

1. Experiencing God is biblical and should be a part of our Christian life. Are there areas where you have been hindering your experience of God? Ask the Lord to begin to reveal those areas.

_____

_____

_____

_____

2. Put some worship music on while reading one verse that inspires you. Pray and meditate on that verse. Then begin to posture yourself, like a sponge, and allow the word and the Spirit of God to saturate you. What did you experience? What did you hear?

_____

_____

_____

_____

[NOTES]

Lesson 15
Walking in the Spirit

"If we live by the Spirit, let us also walk by the Spirit." Galatians 5:25

What does it mean to walk in the spirit? Does it look like asking the Lord everything? Even what we should wear?

I don't think this is what Paul is speaking about, even though some have interpreted this verse that way. Simply put, walking in the spirit is walking in love. Love fulfills the whole law. Instead of living by a set of do's and don'ts, Paul teaches us that choosing love will always lead to the right answer. There are times when the Holy Spirit will speak a very clear word that we are to prophesy, but we may not hear a voice, see a picture or have a dream. Sometimes, like Jesus, we are simply moved by compassion.

For so long we have heard that we should not trust our emotions. This may be true when they are unsanctified, but can the Lord speak through our emotions? Absolutely! Jeremiah was called a weeping prophet. When the word of the Lord came upon Jeremiah, he was moved in his emotions and wept. There are times when I have walked by someone, and I felt moved with compassion (not to be confused with human sympathy). Human sympathy looks at the individual and pities them, with no supernatural cure. Being moved with godly compassion is followed up by divine intervention from the Father.

Being led by God's spirit in love doesn't always look like healing, signs, and wonders. Sometimes it looks like being led by love to listen to someone who needs a friend. I'll never forget when I was at bible school, and I was walking in the supermarket with a friend to get some late night snacks. My friend told an elderly woman there that Jesus loved her. I wasn't prepared for her response. She stopped and said, "You mean someone loves me?" I don't remember if the woman got healed, or even if she said the sinner's prayer, but I do remember her feeling so encouraged that God loved her.

"Pursue love, yet desire earnestly spiritual gifts, but especially that you may prophesy." 1 Corinthians 14:1

We have not only been commanded to love one another, but we are also empowered to love one another according to Romans 5:5, *"the love of God has been shed abroad in our hearts by the Holy Spirit."* My prayer, is that as a generation pursues love, and the gifts of the Holy Spirit, that the nature of Christ will flow through us, bringing a nation to the embrace of a loving Father.

Reflection Questions

1. After reading this lesson, what would you say it means to walk in the Spirit?

_____

_____

_____

_____

2. Why is it so important that we pursue love when we are ministering to other people?

_____

_____

_____

_____

3. *Declaration Prayer: (pray this prayer our loud)*

Beloved Father, I want to love others the way you love me. Fill my cup to overflowing, that out of your love for me, I can love others well for your glory. In Jesus' name!

[NOTES]

_____

_____

_____

_____

_____

_____

_____

_____

_____

_____

_____

_____

_____

_____

_____

_____

_____

_____

_____

_____

_____

_____

_____

_____

_____

_____

_____

THE [HEART OF THE] PROPHETIC

JOURNAL

In this part of the workbook we would like to encourage you to practice hearing the voice of God through journaling. We have included these pages so that you can take the time to sit, listen and journal what you hear God saying. This a practical tool, mentioned in *The Heart of the Prophetic*, that has brought breakthrough for many people, and our hope is that it will do the same for you.

_____
_____
_____
_____
_____
_____
_____
_____
_____
_____
_____
_____
_____
_____
_____
_____
_____
_____
_____
_____
_____
_____
_____
_____
_____
_____
_____
_____
_____

Made in the USA
San Bernardino, CA
02 September 2016